Raised by Wolves

Raised by Wolves

Jim Goldberg

in collaboration with Philip Brookman

The Corcoran Gallery of Art

Addison Gallery of American Art

Zurich Museum of Design

Scalo Zurich – Berlin – New York

Cast of characters

R. Sylvia   COP   GREEN RATHO

ECHO   RHONDA   WILL

~~DAD~~ Tweeky Dave   JILL   MACKI

COOKIE   ~~ABRAM~~ SUGAR DADDY   KATO

RUSTY   MONIQUE   STEVIE KAOS / BRANDY

BLADE   BEAVER   TABITHA

TANK   GIRL   CRYSTAL

LUDGER   COLLEEN   RAY

DARTAK   NICKY PAIN   JOEY

BLOWO BOY   CUTTER   ADAM

STEWART   PATTY   TROY

BAM BAM   CHANCE   SCOOTER

MARCOS   POPS   MAD MAX

BRAD   LORNA   WEZ

DEION   DRONE STEVE   CALVIN

RIVER   CROSS   ANNE-MARIE

DESTINY   IAN BOSTWICK   NIGEL

NAPOLEON   PSYCHO   CASPER

UNIVERSE   RIFF RAFF   MIA

WEA   TINY WALLER   VAMPCHILD

RODNEY   DOCTOR   TORI

JERSEY LU   O.D.   GUSTAVE

HEATHER   MAN   JEFF PHILLIPS

PERRY   WHORE   T.J. a.k.a. TWACK JACK

HIPPIE DAVE   FRANK   AMBER

DARBY   DOUG   PAUL

FRECKIE   KID #1   T.V. TALK SHOW HOST

BON JOVI   KID #2   MALLORY SKIDMORE

VYPER   KID #3   ~~MATILDA~~

RAG DOLL   KID #4   MATILDA WEATHERSBY

MANSON   COUNSELOR   KELLY WALTERS

ZIGGY   PROFESSIONAL   DR. BURSTEIN

PREACHER HILTON   KELLY   DADDY

OFFICER RUBY   DOC   BROTHER IN LAW

MINDY LENNON   ANIMAL   SISTER

Echo's story

*It's winter in the suburbs of New York City. Christmas music is playing on the radio.
I am in a living room, looking at a family's home movies with R. Sylvia, a social worker
at a nearby medical clinic. She is Beth's mother. I first met Beth on the streets of
Hollywood where everyone calls her Echo.*

Jim: She liked horses. Was she a good rider?

R. Sylvia: She only took lessons for one year.

Jim: There she is again. How old is she there?

R. Sylvia: Um, 10. There's her first bicycle. That's my father. That's Beth at
my sister Amy's wedding.

Jim: She's 18 now?

R. Sylvia: Yeah. That's her Aunt Jean. This was Easter Sunday. We had just moved
into this house. She was 13 and was starting to put on a little weight. Right after
her 13th birthday she started running.

Jim: How long has she been gone?

R. Sylvia: You know everything, Jim. She's told you the story. She's been gone
off and on since she was 13. Since October, five years ago. That's when we found
out what had happened to her.

Jim: Where did she go?

R. Sylvia: Usually somewhere close by. One night she slept in a Goodwill
dumpster. She always came back in the morning. Her real father was of no help
to me. We were divorced. He never had a relationship with her. So when I married
her stepfather Ray, who was a very affectionate and very open man, I thought
that was going to solve a lot of problems. And I think she liked him. I looked at
him as a good influence on her life. Of course it didn't turn out that way.

When she was 13, she ran away to the city. We'd been looking
everywhere for her. Her stepfather reassured me that everything would be all right.
And I thought because he was a cop he knew what he was talking about.
She was gone for three days and went to Covenant House. She told them
everything. Once I asked her, "Why didn't you tell anyone before?" And she said,
"Nobody ever asked."

It was around 11:30 at night when the police called. It was the local
department that her stepfather worked for. And they said, "We found Beth. She's
down here with a Child Protective Services worker. Please come and get her."
So we went down there and she was just sitting there. I went crazy. I was so mad
at her I yelled, but I was so glad that she was alive I couldn't stop hugging her.
She just kept smiling this funny little smile and said to me, "I want to talk to Ray
alone." I thought that was strange. But then I thought that she wanted to talk
to somebody who was rational, because whenever she got out of control for

the past year or so, anytime we got in a fight because her room was a mess, he'd go in and calm her down. So I thought that she felt she could talk to him and not to me. So he went into this small room with her. They were in there five minutes or so. The police wired Beth to confront him. She was 13 years old and she wore a wire. They wanted her to get something on tape. Turns out he didn't really say anything incriminating. The only thing he did say was, "You told them, didn't you?" And she said, "Yeah, I did."

When they came out I said, "Okay, we can all go home now." And she said, "I'm not going home." And I said, "What do you mean, you're not?" And Beth said, "Not tonight." She kept trying to tell me something, like I was supposed to read her mind. And I wasn't getting any of it. The CPS worker said, "No, she's really overwhelmed. She's really tired. You can get her in the morning. We'll take her to a youth shelter. She'll be supervised." And I was so tired I just thought, "Oh well...."

We left and Ray said, "I really don't think I can drive." So I drove and about three quarters of the way home he looked like he would pass out. I thought he was having a heart attack. I got him home and he laid down on the bed and said, "I think I feel better. No hospital for me. I'm going to sleep." Five minutes later I heard a knock on the door and it was the cops. It was Ray's lieutenant, plus one of his friends, a detective from the department, and somebody else who I don't remember. And they said, "Yeah, uh, we need to talk to Ray." I thought that maybe he had screwed up on the job. So I went in to wake him up and then I offered the guys some coffee. They said no and went in the living room to wait for Ray. He came out and I saw them all walk out the door together. And I thought, "Shit, he must've really screwed up royally. It's some kind of case he screwed up."

My mother was looking out the window and she yelled, "They're arresting him. They're putting handcuffs on him and putting him into the car." And then it started to click in my mind what it could be about. All the behavior changes, his history, what his father did. I mean, he used to talk about his father in terms of what a monster he was. I thought, "Can't be." So I had to go back down to the station. They put me alone in a room for hours and wouldn't tell me anything. At that time they didn't have the whole story and maybe they thought that in giving his story he would implicate me. Around three o'clock in the morning I asked this detective, "Joe, just tell me one thing. Does this have anything to do with Beth?" He replied, "It looks that way." And I asked, "Is it true?" And he said, "He confessed to it." Then I went crazy for a while. After I calmed down they told me that I could get Beth after a hearing in family court. So I was up all night. By the next afternoon I thought, "I can't handle this."

Jim: Couldn't you get help?

R. Sylvia: I tried. But the system tries to help in such a way that it makes everybody a criminal. Everybody gets screwed over. The next day I went with her

real father to pick up Beth. We waited in a room forever. Her CPS worker never showed his face. I kept asking where he was and when he was coming, and when I was going to get my daughter back. And they said, "Oh yeah, don't worry, he's coming, he's coming." He never showed up.

Jim: What did you do?

R. Sylvia: I finally asked a lawyer, "I don't understand why I can't see my daughter." This lawyer wouldn't answer me. So I started making conversation with one of the Assistant DAs, telling her that I felt that it was important for them to see Beth as a person instead of just as a case to win. I started talking about Beth's background and her high school experiences. Turn's out Beth went to the same Catholic high school that this DA went to. And all of a sudden the DA kind of turned around. It was the first time she saw Beth as a person, as somebody she could relate to. She stopped, looked at me and said, "Yeah, you're right. If it were my daughter I would be very concerned right now." Instantly I got my mind back and this cold chill went up my spine. They were trying to take Beth away from me. That's what this whole thing was about.

Jim: Then what happened?

R. Sylvia: In court the judge said, "Let's move on to document number such and such. This is the motion to make the minor child a ward of the court." Blah, blah, blah. And the county attorney goes, "Yes, the child does not want to return home and the parents have agreed to it." And I went nuts. I screamed, "That's not the case. That's not the case at all." They said, "All right, all right. Let's listen to the attorney. Why don't you sit down."

Then they put my 13 year old daughter in front of all these strangers on the jury to tell a story that she couldn't even tell her mother. And they questioned her and questioned her. The lawyers went on about how they wanted to do what's best for Beth. They said, "Moving her away from her home is the minor's wish and all professional views coincide with this request."

I was about to burst. The judge allowed me to talk and I said, "They asked Beth about this after I had yelled at her because she ran away. I didn't know what had happened. Nobody told me anything. I was reacting to a kid who had put her life in danger by running away. But I did not know what she was running from. I hadn't even had a chance to tell her I loved her or how bad I felt about what happened to her. She made this decision to leave the house not knowing how I felt at all." So then the judge asked, "Is that true? You haven't even let the mother see this girl? Do you have any charges against this woman?" The lawyer said, "Uh, no, we don't. She's been very cooperative." So the judge said, "I'll let you see your daughter, but if she still does not want to go home she will go stay in the shelter. Will you agree to it?"

So they let me see her. And she came home. And I thought, "Okay, this is it. Now things will return to normal." But it was too hard. I had to adjust to losing a husband who I loved and who was never the person I thought he was. It was like he was dead. And I had to adjust to what happened to my daughter: "Is she ever going to be all right again?" Then I had to adjust to the fact that there was no money for anything anymore, because then I only worked part time. Ray left us with a lot of debts. I had to earn a living. And who was going to take care of my kids while I was doing all this? I'm coping with it and they started to send us to every agency and psychologist in the world to make sure that no one was abused. We had to be in court almost every week. They asked me all these questions just to complete their paperwork. There was always another line that had to be filled out. It had nothing to do with helping me or my family or Beth. It was just really tiring. Meanwhile, I was trying to keep a job so I could earn a living. I remember, at one point I was so numb and so stupid that I tried to put my coat on, tried to button it in front of the therapist, and I couldn't get the buttons to work. And finally he said, "I think you have to put your arms in first." I mean that's how stupid I was.

Jim: What happened to Beth?

R. Sylvia: At first it was good she was home. Beth got a lot of attention from my family because everybody felt so bad about what had happened. Then she stopped going to school and refused to see a psychologist. The family court began to intervene. A truant officer came and asked, "Do you want our help getting her to school?" I said, "I can't make her go. I don't know what to do." So he said, "If the parent is unable to exert that kind of authority then sometimes just hearing it from the judge will shape these kids right up." I was stupid enough to believe it. Family court threatened to put her in a shelter if she didn't go to the psychologist or to school.

So she went to school for a while. Then she stopped. We went back to family court and she was sent to a shelter. She ran to the city and they picked her up for prostitution. She denied it. She was 14 and I took her right from the police station to a psychiatric hospital 'cause I felt she was just gonna keep running. She didn't get any help at the hospital either. The only thing they taught her there was how to smoke cigarettes and do a line of cocaine with sugar packets. This was the best hospital in the area and it was highly recommended. It cost $156,000 for eight months. We had insurance but after eight months the insurance ran out and she really wasn't better. She was home for a couple of months and then she started running away to see friends that she knew from the hospital.

One time she was hitchhiking to LA. She made it to Kansas City and they picked her up. We flew her back home. Then she went to court and they sent her to some ridiculous group home. I said, "You can't lock the doors there. What makes you think she's not going to run from there?" It was just a joke. Of course she ran again and fell right into even more trouble. It just snowballed, making everything so much harder. We went back to court and the jackass judge said to Beth, "I think you're gonna be in trouble the rest of your life. But if this is the way you want it, fine, you go home with your mother." All of a sudden she had become a criminal.

Jim: How did Beth react?

R. Sylvia: She stayed here at home for a month and pretty much did what she wanted: slept all day, stayed out all night. She was doing drugs then with her friends. Beth said she wasn't. And part of the reason I believed her was because she was having nightmares. She was very afraid that there was something really wrong. And I was told that very often people who have this fear won't do drugs because it's very scary for them. So I believed her.

One night she called me in to watch a TV talk show. It was that guy with the big mouth. She said she hated him. Got up the next morning and she was gone. Just like that. To California.

Jim: What was the show about?

R. Sylvia: I don't know, rock stars I guess.

I remember once my mother &
father & me ~~went~~ all over ~~[struck out]~~
drove
the country & we saw everything
& anything you could see

It was the best time

We stopped in the middle of
this light green forest

I wandered off & climbed e
tree

Nothin' but bright green everywhere

That was the time my
parents were happiest together

And I was happiest with them

That was the only time I can
remember us being a real family

resent location - 9/21/89

Arrived in CA
5/12/88
- Age 16

5/13/88 - present
- Hollywood streets
S.F.

V.W. Bus trip

step DAD-(ex-cop)
DANNEMORA ST. CORR. FAC.
DOING
C2-5 yrs. For child molesting (For being a
of our
Runaway)

Craig House Hosp. 4/7/86 - 12/10/86

MY home -
mom (childhood - 15 yrs)

BORN
Sea side Hts. - (summer of)
87'

SOMeTIMES reMEMBERING anno ZON

STOP
DO NOT PULL GATE
WAIT TILL IT
BUZZ

NO TRESPASSING
VIOLATORS WILL
BE PROSECUTED

ANY GOODS THAT ARE
IN ROOMS OR IN STORAGE
WILL BE CHARGED $3.00 PER

MANAGER

WARNING
SAN FRANCISCO
PATROL SPECIAL POLICE

OFFICE

NO PETS

NOTICE

VACANCY

ROOMS FOR RENT

ARGUING WITH AN
INSPECTOR
IS LIKE WRESTLING
WITH A PIG
IN THE MUD

ROOM RENT PAID IN ADVANCE
NO VISITERS NO NOISE NO PETS
NO HOT PLATE NO LOITERING
NO ALCOHOL IN THE HALLWAYS
CHECK OUT TIME 8:00 AM NOT
RESPONSIBLE FOR PERSONAL
BELONGINGS LEFT LOST OR
STOLEN FROM THE ROOMS
CHECKING IN TIME 5-6:00 PM
NO REFUND

Oki Dogs, West Hollywood

He's in love. She ain't saying yet. He wants them to die together, "like Sid and Nancy."
That she agrees to. They are dressed like twins: plaid shirts, tank tops, bandannas,
chains, and locks around their necks. He wants to fuck her bad. Echo is now 16,
bleached blond hair. She is with her new "boyfriend," Tweeky Dave. He says he's 16 but
it's hard to tell. He is E.T.-ish, sunken body and eyes. He coughs a lot.

Echo: Dave deals, but not very well. That's what I'm here for. To make sure he
sells it.

Jim: But what if you use it?

Echo: I don't do that, really. I haven't been doing much lately.

Jim: How much do you do?

Echo: Once a week at most. You know, the weekends. Twice a week, maybe, and
that's not even every week. Good tweek ain't been around. And it ain't worth doin'
any ol' stuff just to put a hole in my arm. If there were heroin around I'd do that.
No, I ain't stupid. I want ice cream, Jim. Let's make this an interview with Jim.

Jim: Sorry, but I've been sort of stressing about my book. Where to start?

Echo: Begin at the beginning.

Jim: Do I begin with tweekers or normal suburban kids? Right now it's on abuse
and neglect. But I don't want to make this a straight documentary. I don't think
normal kids are that normal.

Echo: Look, you have this Cosby-type show that people think is going on. Then you
have this horrible family, where people think abused kids are coming from. And
then you have this stuff in the middle, which is where most people are. I'm trying
to think of how you can get the middle part into it. Show little parts of the perfect
family, and then show the horrible nightmare. Maybe use it as a basis, so people
will be more open to seeing the problems with the average kid. There's a kind of
despair that kills that little innocence that kids are supposed to have.

Echo stops talking and goes back to tweeking on her drawings, trying to connect two
imaginary dots, trying to draw a tear coming off a girl's eye. Dave is high on dope and
drinking strawberry tequilas. He tries hard to impress her.

Dave: Baby, I'd do anything for you. I'd treat you good, like the future will always be
with me. Maybe I should go out with that fat faggot, then murphy him for $200 and
give it all to you. I'd do that for you, baby.

Not impressed, Echo is becoming increasingly irritated with Dave's advances.

Echo: Dave, you probably don't even have a dick.

He pulls down his pants. She walks away.

Dave: I love that bitch.

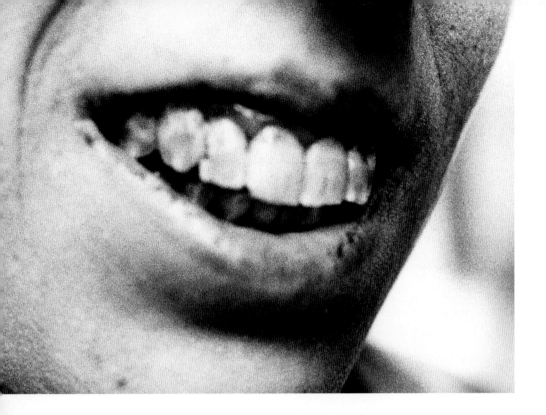

I'M DAve who the FuckAre you

you Need me 2 Feel superior
I Need you 2 LAUghAT

MY MOM WAS A 15 YR OLD JUNKIE SLUT
WHO I AINT NEVER SEEN
MY OLD MAN IS A BIKER FROM HELL

the FUCKed UP ASSHOLE shot me in the
guot WHEN I WAS 1° yrs old
AINT gone home since OR HAD ONE

Dave's story, Hollywood

This is my first time alone with Tweeky Dave. Dave will say "fuck you" when he means he loves you, hug you and give you the shirt off his back.

Broken body saint — ridden hard and put back wet. He is the book. Dave tells me about his life, which doesn't come to much 'cept lies and pain.

Jim: Dave, your life story. Concentrate.

Dave: Fuck that. You know I hate doing this. I had a fucked-up life.
Where do you want to start?

Jim: First memory?

Dave: Slammin' doors and people yelling.

Jim: Any pets?

Dave: Kept a few stray dogs that showed up. They'd hang around for a few days 'til my old man kicked 'em in the teeth. One bit him on the foot once. I laughed.

Jim: What was your mom like?

Dave: A hippie. Deadhead. Stupid, young, sweet.

Jim: How long did you know her?

Dave: 'Til I was about 8 or 9. I don't know. I don't even know who my mom was. There was a chick there for about 5 or 6 years. It was a weird family, dude. This was not "The Brady Bunch."

Jim: What did you do?

Dave: Got beat up a lot. Read a lot. Did a lot of dope.

Jim: How'd you learn to read?

Dave: Like most people. Went to school for a little bit.

Jim: What area of the country?

Dave: Texas. America. California.

Jim: What did your dad do for money?

Dave: Sold dope. Worked on motorcycles.

Jim: And your mom?

Dave: Sold her ass. Did a lot of dope. Sucked dick for wine. I didn't know what it was at the time. She'd go to this bar a few blocks down and come back an hour later with four or five bottles of wine.

Jim: What are your best memories?

Dave: Rock and roll, books.

Jim: What about friends?

Dave: Nah, I'm a loner.

Jim: Describe your house.

Dave: It was gray. It was supposed to be white, but it was gray. It was a shotgun shack, if you know what that is. You could see straight through the front to the back door. Only one room and a porch.

Jim: Food?

Dave: My dad didn't give a shit about food. Baloney and beer and a lot of candy bars. Fuck of a lot of candy bars. My mom did all this heroin so there was a lot of chocolate around. She would tell me to brush my teeth, comb my hair and shit, but it'd be like every five or six days.

Jim: Were they dirty?

Dave: My mom was just this dirty flower child. My dad was just this greasy biker. I shoulda died from hepatitis. Fuck, we're all gonna die, so if I die from toothaches, fuck it. I don't particularly want to die. I'm not on a suicide mission. There's a lot of responsibility livin' on the street man. I'm takin' care of a lot of brothers and sisters now. And now I gots Echo.

Jim: Violence at home?

Dave: Butt fucking, okay? Rape.

Jim: Dad or mom?

Dave: She was too fucked-up to screw him, much less me. That's probably why he fucked me.

Jim: What did they do when you played with their needles?

Dave: My old man used to trip out 'cause he'd figured out that I'd figured out what to do with them. And my old lady, she'd go, "Oh that's cute." Dude, you know what heroin is when you're like 5, and you watch someone stick a needle in their arm and then go puke, it's fucked-up.

Jim: Did you watch TV?

Dave: When it wasn't in the pawn shop for dope.

Jim: No memories of hugs?

Dave: Dude, I was cynical from birth. I knew what was up. Maybe that's why I can deal with it now. I cut myself off from whatever's happening around me. They told me I was retarded 'cause I could do that. My old man said, "Well, you're a retarded faggot." That was cool 'cause I'd tell him right back, "You keep sticking your dick in my ass, maybe I am a faggot."

Jim: Why did he rape you?

Dave: I'm not a fucking psychologist, man.

Jim: Did anyone help?

Dave: Fuck no, man. Which is why I'll never have a kid. I'm fucked-up enough. I'm not gonna fuck somebody else's life up. I don't know, I might be a hell of a parent. Listen, if I could find Echo right now I might change my mind.

Jim: How did you survive?

Dave: Rode bikes a lot. Stole my first bike when I was 8.

Jim: So where'd you go on the bike? Do you remember trees?

Dave: Couple of real skinny ones. I'd ride everywhere. I just rode man. I didn't have directions. I was free. Then when I turned 9 I got hip to hitchhiking. It was then that I found out you could make a profit at it. Fuck it, if you're gonna get fucked in the ass you might as well make fifty bucks. I went to juvenile hall a couple of times for running away.

Jim: Where would you go?

Dave: Like 7-Eleven. I was 7 years old, man. I'd run away to play pinball. After about eleven p.m. the guy would go, "Why don't you go home, Dave?" And I'd go, "Fuck you." So he'd call the cops and they'd come and tell me to go home and I'd go, "Fuck you, you can take me to jail. I'm not going home." So they'd take me to the station and call my dad. Sometimes he'd come and beat the shit out of me. And sometimes he wouldn't come at all, probably thinking to himself, "Fuck the kid, let him rot."

Jim: Any church people come around?

Dave: No. I didn't start going to church 'til I was 14 or 15. Out here in California. Thought I'd find God. Then I realized God was either too busy or didn't give a shit. I decided people fuck with God too much. They put too much shit on his head, man. I'm not gonna bother with God and I hope he don't bother with me too much. I've had preachers tell me, "Dave, you could be the greatest thing on earth, save so many souls." And I'm like, "Aw, let's shoot some crack instead."

Jim: When did you create this whole mythology of Tweeky Dave?

Dave: I do it as I go along. I've always had a fantastic imagination, plus a perspective on where I'm at.

Jim: Why make things up?

Dave: 'Cause it's better than the truth. It doesn't hurt as much. I'd just make up stories about myself, like I was a cowboy and goin' off and fuckin' robbing and shit. I was always into that. Fuckin' Billy the Kid and Jesse James and shit. I think that's where a lot of this persona of Dave comes from. I went from being Billy the Kid to being a guitar slammer to being a junkie. That way I don't need a fucking psychiatrist. I already told them to just leave my head alone.

Jim: Why did you become a junkie if your parents were?

Dave: I like dope. My first experience with dope was great, man. I got high and didn't care if people were yelling and screaming at me.

Jim: When? How old were you?

Dave: 6, 5 maybe. My dad held me down and slammed it, mostly to shut me up. He'd beat me and I'd bitch. I'd ask stupid questions like, "Why'd you hit me? Do you hate me?" That was a big question. He'd tell me shit like, "I hate everybody, why should you be any different?"

Jim: Do you know where he is now? What if he comes to you now and says, "Dave, I love you"?

Dave: I'd say, "Suck my dick." Dude, I don't wanna get into all this. I told you, let's just drop it. I got to find Echo. She needs me. She's real insecure. She said she would probably fuck me if I grew my hair long. I got to find her.

August 18, Plummer Park, West Hollywood

Echo is crashing in Plummer Park with her new boyfriend The Magician. Her hair is dyed black. She talks tough but shows me her broken finger and tells me how a girl with a large screwdriver did it, and how some other chick tore out one of her earrings. Echo is now missing the bottom half of her ear lobe. It forms an upside-down V.

Echo: It's not a game anymore. There is nowhere to go, the street is my home. Dave is immature and I won't talk to him.

Next day

Dave and I cruise Hollywood Boulevard looking for Echo. He heard she broke up with The Magician.

Dave: Echo thinks she's a bad-ass bitch, but this girl Patty said fuck you to that shit. That was one of the best fights I've ever seen. Patty knows what street fighting is about. But Echo, she put up some heart, man.

Looking behind him, suddenly Dave screams.

Dave: Hot lips, finger tips.

He sees Cookie, this cute little girl with a snugly bear dangling from her bag and a cap turned backwards. Cookie is like the kid who just got back from a baseball game with her dad, except for the graffiti written all over her pocketbook:

Live Fast and Die Tweeking

Cookie loves Nikki, Nikki, Nikki, Nikki

fuck peace

Tweeks-4-ever.

Cookie tells everyone that I'm her personal photographer. She says she does modeling and signed a contract to do a movie.

Dave: Porno?

Cookie: Nah. Rated R. Nudity in it though. Gonna make $400.

Cookie was promised a job dancing by the guy who owns the "family restaurant" down on the Boulevard. All she had to do was sit on his lap and snort cocaine — she didn't have to fuck him either. The guy gave her an advance, so now she is looking for tweek. She promises to give Dave a quarter of a gram if he'll help her find some.

Dave: Cool.

They are on a mission to get high. Dave temporarily forgets about Echo and is contorting his body with a lust for drugs. Looking for dope is more fun than finding it. We drive to Oki Dogs, then Donut Time, and back to the Boulevard. Nothing.

Cookie switches clothes with a friend who has a date. Now she is dressed more like a whore. They find Pops, who has heroin, and Cookie stuffs it in her underwear.

Dave: I don't care, the veins can't smell pussy.

Nothing I would say or do could interrupt their addiction. They need more money for a point. At Oki Dogs, Cookie hustles $20 from an older man.

Cookie: C'mon daddy, it's for rent, or else my big black roommate will bust my legs.

At the corner they find this guy tweeking in a bush who knows an old queen who might know someone in Plummer Park who maybe has points. He will show us. We walk half way in, spot cops, turn around. They pull us aside, spread our legs, twist our arms behind our backs, shit. They take the guys away in a squad car and let me off because I convince them I am a photographer. They put me in charge of the minor, Cookie.

As I drive her back to Nikki Pain's hotel room at the Sunset Palms, Cookie pulls out the tweek and tells me her plan to slam the whole amount into her neck as soon as she can find Nikki.

Cookie: I'm sorry for Dave but I gots to do this dope. I'm too stressed and I can't wait.

I leave her off at the corner.

August 20, Oasis alley

Dave is out from jail.

Dave: It wasn't bad, man. They only broke a couple of ribs.

It's Tuesday, Oasis shelter night, which means free food, clothes, lots of sermons, and bad Jesus-wanna-be rock and roll. Dave trades in what he's wearing and re-emerges as a skin-tight-pink-velour-pants, torn-t-shirt (open to his chest), bandanna (falling over his eyes), metal-studded-bracelet, black-boots (untied and at least four sizes too big), mascara-rubbed-under-eyes, black-faced-rock-and-roll-star. Dave hears Echo is looking for him. He thinks she is jealous and that she must love him. Once she finds him, they walk away and his arm is on her shoulder. He is leaning over, trying to convince her how much he loves her. Dave keeps saying he is "indicated" and Echo tells him she can't handle the stress. Late night Hollywood Boulevard is a conveyor belt of equally-distant heads-lowered lonely people. Daydreaming.

At three a.m. I am driving down the Boulevard and see a girl who looks like Cookie, handcuffed, busted for selling dope hidden in a baby carriage. The lights of the cop car illuminate the girl, and her glazed-over eyes, half dead, are brought momentarily back to life.

things
2 Do tomorrow
Get high!
see echo
see jim
see mishka
eat maybe
maybe sleep?
tweeky dave!

the old MAN WAS covered with tattooes
AND scars — got some in prison others in Bars
the rest He got workin on JUNK cars
IN the DAY time —
the NEIghbors said We lived like hicks
But they BRing their cars & Pa to fix any how
If that aint country it will HARE LIP the POPE
If that aint country its a damn good joke
Iseen the grand old opry I met Jhonny cash
If that aint country I'll kiss your ASS
MY MAMA sells eggs IN a grocery store
and
MY little sister is a first RATER whore and
daddy said she cant come home NO more and he
and I left home cause he got violent and he means it
If that aint country I'll hare lip the pope
If that aint country its a damn good joke
cause I seen the grandol opry an I met
JOHNNY CASH IF that aint country I'll KISS yei ass

4650 Sunset Boulevard

Post Office Box 54700

Los Angeles, California 90054-0700

213/660 2450

June 6, 1990

Jim Goldberg
1007 Gaight Street, #3
San Francisco, CA 94117

Dear Jim:

I'm responding to your inquiry about Dave Miller and his contact with our High Risk Program at the Los Angeles Free Clinic. Dave, or "Tweeky Dave", as he is known on the street, has a very complex past history which involves substance abuse, suicide attempts, homelessness and multiple other risk taking behaviors. As is all too common, he presented to our program with a medical complaint. His bronchitis produced a discomfort severe enough to seek out medical care. At that time, the complicating factors of his past and present lifestyle greatly contributed not only to his physical but psychological and social dysfunction.

We made an attempt to develop an integrated plan for management of his total health needs, but the lack of followup on his part diminished our ability to help. It is not unusual for these young people who have adopted the culture of the streets as their society, and the friendships established as their family, to find difficulty in following through with any interventions which are attempting to make a transition in their lifestyle. It is our understanding from our contacts and outreach workers that Dave continues to live a life characterized by impulsive behaviors to satisfy his day to day needs. He has initiated no further contacts with our clinical staff.

Sincerely,

Richard G. MacKenzie, MD, Director
Division of Adolescent Medicine

Associate Professor of Pediatrics
  and Medicine
University of Southern California
School of Medicine

RGM:c

It's Not Like you Can go Home And watch TV

  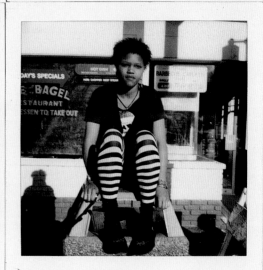

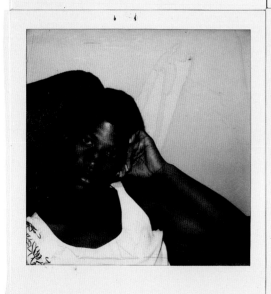 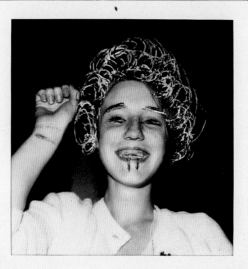 

I've known a couple of kids who lied about what their parents did to them

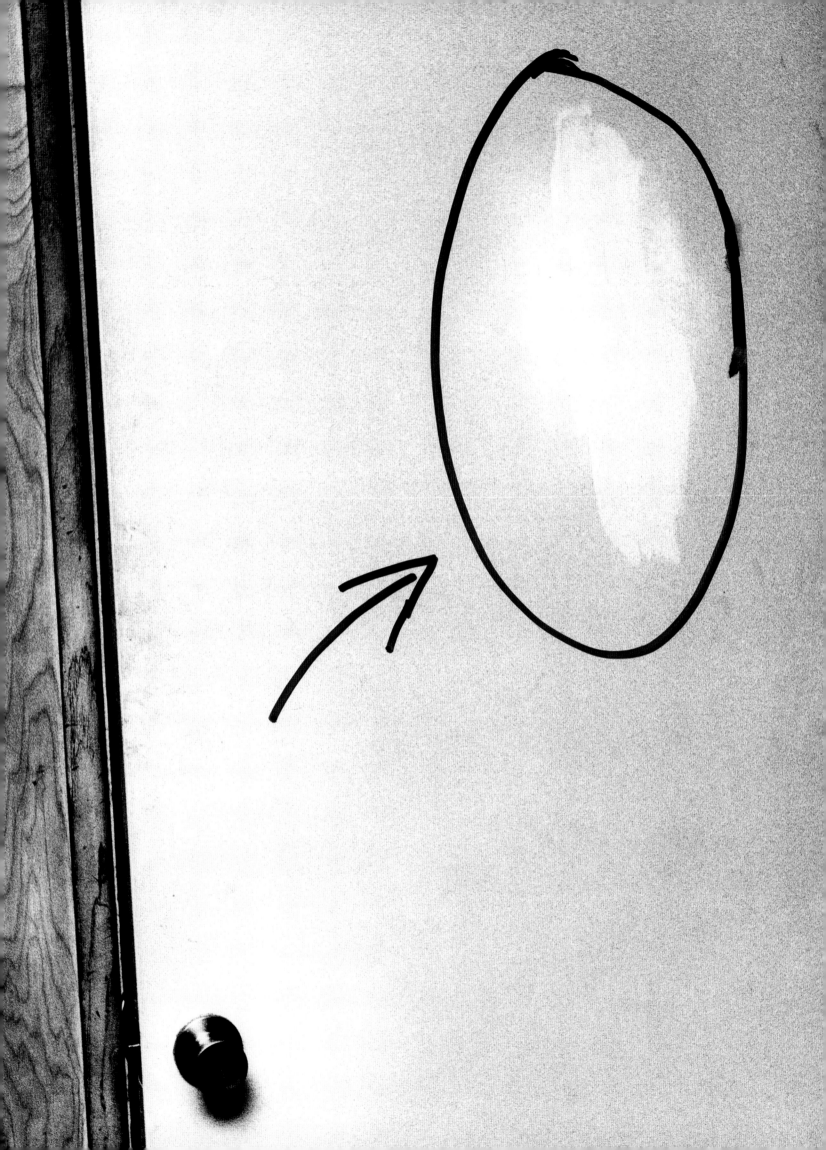

I ran away from home
my dad hit me

my mom abandon me

It was all my fault
I was a bad kid
I'm a born loser
a peace of shit

I want to die
NOW !!

bridge of death

RUSTY BOY

Infinity is pure chance,
not god, and what is chance?
It's myself, I was told by myself
who listens to me. And I answered myself:
All my selves are there because
as far as I'm concerned,
I am not listening to you.

NO LOITERING

WE RESERVE THE   NOT RESPONSIBLE
RIGHT TO REFUSE   FOR ARTICLES LEFT
SERVICE TO ANYONE HERE

REST
FOR
ON

Rusty, San Francisco

One day in the Haight, some sad-faced guy named Rusty comes up to me hustling
for money.

       Rusty: Do you want to buy a leather?

His friend Aaron is a few feet away, panhandling change for acid. He wants to get enough
to buy a fifty dose sheet and then sell it for two bucks a hit. He says he can make $50
a day, plus it's fun, plus he gets a free fry. The next time I run into Rusty
he's at Civic Center. He is badly sunburned, depressed, and shaken.

       Rusty: I've just seen my mom comin' down the street, smilin' and shit. And
       I go, it's like a fuckin' movie. I mean, I hadn't seen her in a while and we got high
       together. She gots a new boyfriend. Now she lives in Washington state, gots
       a horse and a Harley. She likes speed a lot. Came down to party for the weekend.
       She promised me a home but she went into some bar and I lost her. Guess when
       things get too happy for me then it's time for it to get bad again.

Rusty pleads with me to turn him in to the cops so that he would have a roof over his
head. He whispers, as if it's a secret, that he's scared.

       Rusty: Yesterday morning I was cruising this squat, looking for a place to crash
       and to take a shit, and something smells like fuck. I think it's cool, it's through
       this door, so I went in and I see this dead body, alls black and blue. I took Aaron
       there to see it. Now where am I goin' to stay? I don't want to end up like Aaron,
       suckin' some guy's dick for a hotel room. There are always dudes that'll offer
       me a place to stay to get down my pants. I know I'm a stud but I got my pride.
       And anyways, I likes girls. So that's why I'm burnt like fuckin' toast. Walkin' around
       tryin' to figure out how to survive. It's like, I get to the point where I'm like, uh,
       when's it gonna end?
       Jim: How long do you think you're gonna live?
       Rusty: 'Til about 20. Someone's gonna come up behind me and stab me or shoot
       me. If I return, I'll come back as a bird — that's what I want. To come back as an
       eagle and swoop down on my prey.

Again, Rusty offers me his leather. He is desperate for money. I ask him if it was
stolen and he says, "No." We make a deal. I let him and an Indian girl stay in the back
of my truck. I scrape the nihilistic punk text off the back and go out, heading for Powell
and Market. Some little punk named Rabbit is there, complaining to this big skin named
Animal, about how some punk asshole named Rusty had stolen his leather jacket.
I walk the other way.

One week later, Golden Gate Park

Rusty: C'mon Jim Goldberg, you major fanatic. Don't walk like they walk, like the Egyptian.

In a circle of trees, Rusty is with a new girl, Dawn. They have beer and he's happy. He and Aaron are toasting to the "Beer Gods." Dawn sits on Rusty's lap. She can't be more than 13. Two other boys, Wheatberry and Romeo, are there. They're maybe 12. They are trying to smoke cigarettes in order to look older but are coughing a lot. They still have homes and parents — just weekend warriors, for now.

Rusty: This is what I dream about: havin' a girl, havin' her enjoy me, being surrounded by all my buddies, and me enjoyin' them. Like yesterday, I bought $35 worth of meat, made a fire in the park, and gave everybody a barbecue. I earned a lot of people's respect. That was cool. It's like the Bible said about sharing and shit. Like we're all family.

Aaron: Yeah, I know what you mean. There was this girl's baby who died, and everyone's walking around all sniveling and shit and I wasn't. I mean, I'm just following the rainbow.

Rusty: I want to get my jacket back from you, Jim. Get it worked on. Get some new shoes, a new tat. Then I'd be set. Maybe fly down to Hawaii. Work. Buy some bud and bring it back and make some real bucks. None of this chump nickel-and-dime shit.

Aaron: Dude, you must've had a bad dream last night. You kept screaming, "No, no, get off me. Not that, no I can't. I never done that."

Rusty: Fuck you.

Aaron: Fuck you, you did.

Three days later

Rusty calls repeatedly from a youth shelter. He needs to talk to me. Finally we connect on the street.

Rusty: They kicked me out of the housing program because I didn't make curfew. This asshole counselor kicked me out. He didn't like me. I'm an asshole, he's an asshole.

Jim: Maybe you should go apologize.

Rusty: I'm not going back to that asshole. It ain't gonna work. If it were meant to be, if it weren't for him, it might've worked. Shit, this is supposed to be a program for kids on the street, right? Well, you think kids on the street are walking around with halos on their heads? Apologize for what? Having an asshole counselor? Having no father and a junkie mother? Sure, I'll apologize for swearing in front of him 'cause he was busting my ass and I couldn't take it no more. That's it, I'm like a time bomb. I'm gonna explode.

Aaron: Say, I hear they're giving job interviews for the carnival. I'm gonna get me a shower and go for it. Get a free meal at the youth shelter. What d'ya say? Want to come?

The two go off skipping.

The phone rings, 2:30 a.m.

Jim: Rusty, it's late.

He is confused — crying one minute, screaming at me the next.

Rusty: I'm afraid I will go numb and then I swear I'll kill somebody.

Jim: Rusty, it might be a good idea if you control your anger.

Rusty: Why should I?

One week later, a phone message

Rusty: Hello, this is Rusty and I'm in juvie. I need my shit. I socked a cop. I didn't do nothing, I swear. So they're gonna send me back to Seattle without my shit 'cause they don't give a damn about me. You might think it's just bullshit 'cause it's juvenile, but it's still lockup. You got no freedom. It sucks 'cause there's a little room with a big metal door and a bed. They got a toilet at the end of the hall and you gotta bang on your door 'til a security guard lets you out to go. Then he stares at you while you sit there. All I can think about is that I want a cigarette so fuckin' bad. I hope you bring me my shit. So, if I don't see you, well, I'll drop you a letter or two. Take care, Jim Goldberg. Sincerely, James Russell — Rusty.

Blade and Tank, Hollywood

There is a small house converted to a medical building. In the back, garbage is everywhere: a burned-out, thrashed pick-up, an old Chevy packed full with junk, etc. There is another small house all the way at the end. Examining rooms? I go in through a door and a hallway. Graffiti. I try to sound tough. "Hey!" No answer. To the left, a bathroom. Toilet stuffed-up, spilling over. The floor is covered with food, clothes, and shit. There is partially burned toilet paper hanging on a pock-marked shower curtain. A trail of butts leads from the bathroom, to the next room, to a big hotel ashtray, cigarettes spilling all over. There are two mattresses, one with graffiti sprayed on it, blankets disheveled. On the other mattress the blankets are folded, hospital-style, corners tucked in perfectly. The wall above them is covered with the words "sick of it all — good-bye," spray-painted on a blanket draped over the window, like a giant moth. Below are empty matchbooks and decapitated lighters, crushed cans, a German beer stein, a Vienna Sausage can, opened, and a newspaper. The headline: "Cries of Bias in Death of Youth at Hands of Law." In the closet are crumpled pants, one shoe, and a book titled "Personal Bible: Verses of Comfort, Assurance, Salvation." The walls are covered with Nazi slogans, a few jokes, and a dialogue between two tweekers. Back out to the left, in the main room, a table is piled high with old rations, fast food wrappers, graffiti on everything. Empty milk cartons, beer cans, and bottles. Bugs. Red soda syrup spilled all over. Take-out containers. The floor is covered the same way. A couch is littered with butts. Ceiling total graffiti. Overturned furniture, burned walls, comics, porno mags, a blanket with two pairs of black boots. A quick "Hey!" I meet Blade and Tank.

Blade is unique. She is a 16 year old actress-wanna-be. She could be the star if this were a movie. Her real name is Mickey. She is dark. She wants to become emancipated from her parents and have Tank's baby by the time she is 17. Tank is 23, pot-bellied from all his dumpster diving success. A big talker, he is the "older guy" who hangs out with younger kids so he'll be cool. They are in love and they kiss a lot. They also compete a lot.

> **Blade:** I can do a fuck of a lot more doses than you, dude.
>
> **Tank:** Ah shit, girl. I don't get off on those bunk doses.
>
> **Blade:** Oh, fuck you. If I want to hallucinate I do STP.
>
> **Tank:** Girl, you don't know shit about drugs.
>
> **Blade:** Fuck you I don't. When I was 3, I had my first joint. And when I was 6, I was doing my first doses.

We split. I buy them cigs and hair spray for his mohawk. We head for the old Errol Flynn estate-turned-squat up the hill. Hopping a fence, Tank says the guardhouse is the place for satanic rituals. He shows me the candles and porno mags. Plastic sheeting. A sleeping bag. Further up a winding path I hear giggles. "Who goes there?" "What's the secret password?" Introductions. There is Ludger, a ska rasta who is not very talkative, and Tartak, a.k.a. Albert Pease. Everybody says he can eat more than anyone else.

Blade: How'd you get that name?

Tartak: I can lift up concrete like Tartak in the Marvel comic.

Richard and Jennifer from North Carolina are peace punks wearing Sid Vicious t-shirts and Birkenstocks. Hippie Dave is pissing in a bush. And Darby, who doesn't say much, has his hand in his pants. They are all fed up with the Hollywood squats and the cops, and are trying to get back to the earth up here in the hills.

Blade: Fuck sleeping out. There are things out here at night that howl at the moon.

Ludger: I know what they are, mon. They are dead movie stars and their dead dogs, moaning by the empty swimming pool.

Tank: Don't worry. I like things that creep up on me. I was hitching someplace. Got a ride. When I woke up I was in El Salvador and was hired as a mercenary. I killed a lot of people. Check this out. Imagine a bass line…shotgun drums… guitar layover…. Oh what she'll do for my rock and roll machine…is show me things that I ain't never seen ….

They all make a list of their favorite band names:

1 *Saneless Steel*

2 *Original Sin*

3 *Wargasm*

4 *Bad Attitude*

5 *Shakur Down (or Shaker Down)*

6 *Worship (or Warship)*

7 *Lusteel*

8 *Cooked Alive*

9 *Rockway w / Jimmi O. Zone*

10 *Spaded Ace*

11 *Regurgitated Afterbirth (punk!)*

We split down the hill to the Boulevard (Avenue of the Stars). Blade and Tank stop (always) at Bela Lugosi's star and suck each others' neck. Kiss. We go to the youth shelter. Mostly there are a bunch of hustlers, punks, and plaid-shirted-metal-head Bon Jovis sitting around, bumming cigs. BORED. Waiting. The first kid I meet asks what he would get for helping me. His name is York and he snuggles next to Teddy Bear. Then I meet a girl called Angel and next to her, Robert. Angel is giving Robert a hand job under his coat. A boy asks anyone who is gay to raise their hand. One kid forces Blond Boy's small hand up. He air fights with a karate chop and swears he's not gay.

Blond Boy: I heard that the street is a dangerous place where people get hurt and have sex and get transplants.

It was loud

Going down fast. A six foot guy with long blond hair, wearing a Led Zeppelin shirt and studded bracelet, keeps looking at me and calling me dude in a shrill, teenager sort of voice. His name is Dude. "Dude, are you fucking gay?" Nasally snickering. Stewart has many pimples and a long Mohawk sticking up ten inches. He tries to take Bam Bam's seat and gets kicked. Stewart says I ought to smell him. One girl pulls out a big knife, denounces all her detractors, and warns some outside enemy that she means business. Then a loud argument erupts about which is better, the Army or the Air Force.

>**Stewart:** Anyway, the Air Force is no good 'cause what if you were smoking reefer with some nigger in a cockpit and you started to fall?
>
>**Bam Bam:** Who gets laid more?
>
>**Stewart:** If you could make it to your eighteenth without a record, the Army and the Marines would straighten you out. I could go to college and get benefits.
>
>**Bam Bam:** And you get to blow up things.
>
>**Blond Boy:** Well, if we all believed in peace we wouldn't need no Air Farce.
>
>**Stewart:** Shut the fuck up. You couldn't even keep your faggot boyfriend from beating you up.

Later, San Francisco

Deion is in tight, tight pants with his zipper down. He swings his way around me and on down the street, twirling and flirting with everything in sight. He brags that he is the best to be found and will do anybody, anywhere, any time, to reach his dream, which is to be crowned the prettiest drag queen in San Francisco. He thinks the way he's going to get there is by smoking his way to the top with rock cocaine.

Deion dances into a guy. Handshake. Something's passed. Another handshake. He crosses the street. He hugs a young couple and tries to squeeze the girl's ass. She hits him lightly. He shoots up the block and meets up with a big guy who slightly tilts his shades. They argue. Deion runs across the street again to this tall, bare-chested, plaid-shirt-tied-around-his-waist, zipper-half-way-down, cross-around-his-neck rocker-kid who is kissing an older, well-dressed man. Deion puts his hand out. Something passed again. Deion licks the old guy's face. He tongues (hard) the rocker-kid. I enter another world.

Marcos, Polk Street

I meet up with Marcos at an all night restaurant. He is about my height, black, with one eye going off in the wrong direction. His teeth are not great. His hair is greased heavily and combed up and back into a pompadour and he wears loafers without socks. He calls himself "The Ugly Duckling." He is with Brad who is very quiet. Marcos seems buzzed, happy, and definitely loud, trying to sell a combo TV/cassette/radio to the waitress. Marcos snaps his fingers and says "boom boom" a lot. He is close to my face and snaps to my eyes.

> **Marcos:** I graduated a year early from high school. Boom, boom. My mother dominated me. Boom, boom.

Snap. Snap.

> **Marcos:** She tried to drown me down a bathtub. Slapped. Beat. Extension cords. Boom, boom.

Snap.

> **Marcos:** I left after my brother raped me. Boom, boom. I'm scared of black men and women.

Snap. Snap.

> **Marcos:** It's not like I can go home and walk the dog. Boom, boom. I miss my grandmother so much. I loved that woman.

Snap.

> **Marcos:** I want to go to City College and take acting classes and be normal. Boom.

Snap. Snap. Snap.

> **Marcos:** You know, the biggest problem is that grown-ups don't know whether they are kids or adults. Sometimes the roles are all fucked-up.

Brad rolls his eyes. He is not convinced. I pay the bill. Brad reminds the waitress about the "home entertainment center," and that they could let it go for $10 'cause he doesn't want to carry it home. No answer.

> **Brad:** How 'bout $5.

We all go out on the street. Every ten feet or so Marcos and Brad stop and hug a new group of boys and girls, while simultaneously looking over their shoulders for some bad memory or a cop who might be following them. These few blocks are where the younger hustlers hang, those who command the highest prices of $50 or $75, or maybe, maybe $100. They are the ones who aren't spent-up yet. After you turn 18 you are pushed toward the bargain basement area which is only a few blocks away. Kids rarely can see beyond the hype and (drugged) fog to become conscious of their sad future of $20 tricks.

Deion comes up and tries to hug Brad but Marcos interferes and pushes him away.
A minor scuffle.

Marcos: Jim, girl, boom, boom, can I tell you something? I love Brad, and I will never let that girl get near my boy, Brad.

Snap, snap. Deion throws off Marcos's insult.

Deion: I'm so fine, Miss Thang, I made $250 for just sitting in a Jacuzzi and jacking this daddy off. Then I just lay on the bed and watched a porno and let him suck my dick. Got fucked-up good and got free food. See, this guy, he cares about me. He's helping me to know the right people. You know, the ones that take young boys on vacations and stuff. His friend Dennis has a plane. I swear, Miss Thang, there's a future in this business when you got brains and a body like mine. After all, I got more money than you got hair on your balls. My parents live in Beverly Hills and I'm goin' home tonight.

Late night, Hollywood

River: I'm majoring in drool. And I'm feeling good 'cause I been baggin' pot for these old hippies. I made $14 and they got me stoned and gave me food.

Jim: You got parents?

River: I left 'cause I didn't want to mow the lawn. No shit, I couldn't handle the stress of their rules no more. They told me they were sick of my actions. They said, "If that's what you want then that's what we'll give you." They drove me out to the freeway on-ramp and dropped me off. I aimed for Hollywood straight-up. Once in a while I hang with the punk rockers but I don't like what they stand for — chaos, anarchy, disorder. Lately I'm standing behind the Aryan Nation skins. 'Cept I'm just not into all their Hitler stuff.

River is with three giggly skin girls who are singing, "I just want my skin boy to keep me warm, hold me tight, and beat me right." The skin girls are all tired of wandering. I go with them to a new squat I had heard about, a metal-grated fire escape next to an old theater. Angela (now dead) and Cornell (metal plate in head — hasn't been sober since) are at the top, drunk. Puppet is trying to fuck Michelle on the flat grating below. Dana is asleep, covered by a blanket. The three skin girls are still giggling, excited 'cause they've decided to "steal Nigger Dana's blanket so we can have us a sleep over party." Cornell feeds Michelle liquor. Puppet fucks Michelle while Cornell is singing:

> *"Ring a ding doo,*
> *What the hell is that?*
> *All soft and brown, like a pussycat.*
> *Well, she invited me into her bedroom*
> *to get a taste of that ring a ding doo."*

River decides there's nothing for him here and splits to the Boulevard. Tweeky Dave is there, looking for Echo. He hasn't seen her for days. His arms are flapping from speed. He is biting his chapped lips bloody from concentrating so hard, thinking about her. He heard she was at Oki Dogs and, not slowing down, he's on his way to find her.

Dave: I'm a junkie for her man. If I'm goin' after something, stop signs and red lights ain't in my way. Caution lights are just rushin'. Every now and then in life I just gotta say fuck it, I'm gonna go.

Walking around for hours and hours
and not being able to stop

Freezing all the time - exhausted, dazed

After two weeks I didn't even remember why I ran away

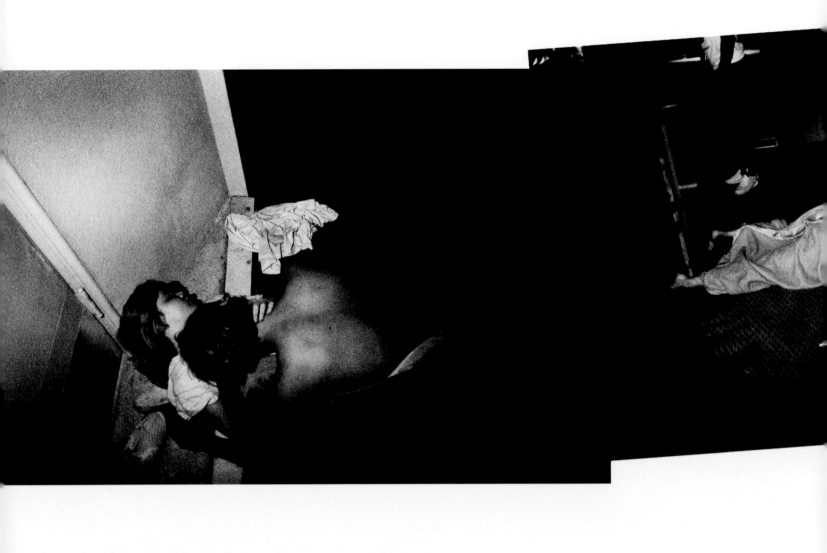

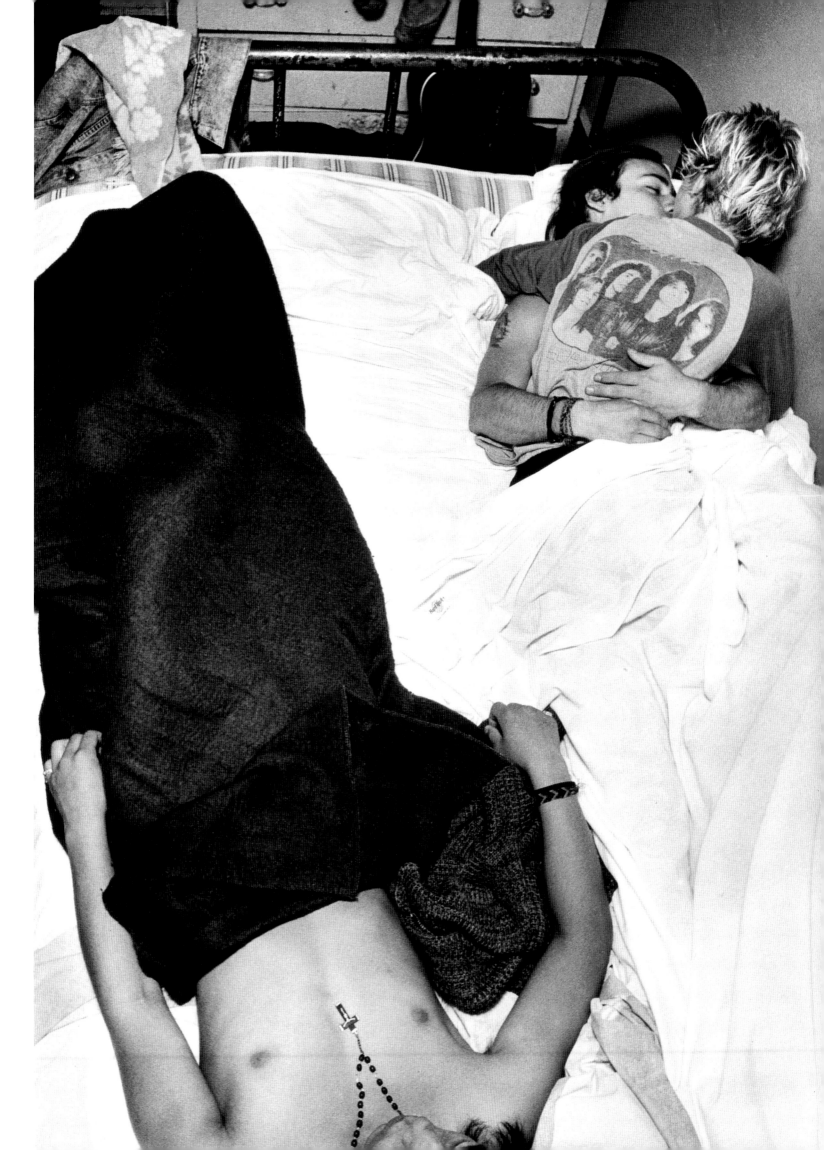

Friday?

♡ Dad,

I'm really sorry about losing control of myself + hurting you (+ the, ahem, bathroom mirror).

I know + understand that talk doesn't mean a damn thing to you by now. (Especially from my mouth.) I don't blame you?

You were right. I _was_ of line, but you really hurt my feelings because I guess I've felt ignored

REQUEST FOR ENFORCEMENT OF
TRESPASS AND DOORWAYS IN ABSENCE OF OWNER OR AGENT

647(i) PC — Every person who commits any of the following acts is guilty of disorderly conduct, a misdemeanor; who lodges in any building, structure, vehicle or place, whether public or private, without the permission of the owner or person entitled to the possession or in control thereof.

602(l) PC — Entering and occupying real property or structures of any kind without the consent of the owner, the owner's agent, or the person in lawful possession.

602(n) PC — Refusing or failing to leave land, real property, or structures belonging to or lawfully occupied by another and not open to the general public, upon being requested to leave by peace officer at the request of the owner/agent, or the person in lawful possession, and being informed by the peace officer that he/she is acting at the request of the owner/agent. The owner/agent, or person in lawful possession shall make a separate request to the peace officer on each occasion when the peace officer's assistance in dealing with a trespass is requested. A single request for a peace officer's assistance may be made to cover a limited period of time not to exceed 30 days and identified by specified dates. In addition, a single request for peace officer's assistance may be made for a period not to exceed 6 months when the premise/property is closed to the public and posted as being closed.

602(s) PC — Entering upon private property, including contiguous land, real property, or structures thereon belonging to the same owner, whether or not generally open to the public, after having been informed by a peace officer at the request of the owner/agent or the person in lawful possession, that the property is not open to the particular person; or refusing or failing to leave the property upon being asked to leave the property in the manner provided.

To the SAN FRANCISCO POLICE DEPARTMENT,

I hereby request that the San Francisco Police Department enforce the above Penal Code Sections on my behalf and in my absence. I have given no person(s) permission to sleep, lay, or in any way remain within my doorway located at   16 Turk Street
(private property) while my business is closed.   25 Mason Street

I further state that I will notify the San Francisco Police Department in writing within 24 hours if I do give person(s) permission to sleep, lay, or in any way remain within said doorway with said person(s) name.

I agree to post a copy of this notice in such a location so as to be visible to person(s) or public within said area. I understand that this letter of request expires in 6 months of the below signed date.

SIGNATURE OF OWNER OR AGENT: _____

DATE: _____ May 13, 1991 _____

ADDRESS: _____ 45 McAllister Street _____

2 Copies: SFPD
          Owner

AGENT TO POST

Highway 101, under the Hollywood Freeway

A notice for a missing child is pasted on the concrete monument of the overpass. I criss-cross the freeway entrance, jump a fence, run down a hill on the left. Below into the blackness where the fires are going there are perhaps thirty people living in pandemonium. In the middle of it all sits a stripped-down motorcycle that has become an altar to the trash. Next to it, shopping carts. In one there is a can of lighter fluid, a home-sweet-home sign, and a broken mirror. In another is dead grass. Someone put an eye — a red button — in the middle of it. The sole of a shoe stands in as a mouth. They call it "the dinosaur" and they like to play with it.

On another part of the wall they write mixed tags. I recognize Tank's scrawl, "You choose Jesus or Satan, Heaven or Hell, Life or Death — I chose free will for all." Next to the altar is a wall of retablos, prayers in Spanish. Plastered to the rest of the wall are pin-up girls, attacked and scratched off until the swastikas drawn underneath shine through. The lucky kids get beds built into mounds of dirt with bankrupt mattresses. Others maybe sleep on a dirty blanket or right in the dirt. Destiny and Napoleon are naked, fucking. Destiny calls out to me. She wants to pose for my camera.

> **Destiny:** My uncle used to take photos of me all the time. You know, bikinis and naked stuff. Then he'd give me things.

Napoleon is embarrassed. Destiny leaves to fuck some biker for food and a place to stay inside. Napoleon plays chicken, flying freely, falling. All the others are getting high or trying to sleep one off. Happy talk. Singing. Marvin and Stony Beth are passed out on top of each other. Quiet time here in Hollywood.

Oki Dogs

Marcos and Brad are in Hollywood, hiding out from Brad's boyfriend, Troy. Marcos says Brad loves him now. He stands on a chair and vows to protect and love him 'til the end. He breaks into song:

> **Marcos:** Love. There is a certain type of love that we share. And it's the truest if it's really there. It's the love between a man and a man. No parts to play, the roles have gone away. It's you loving me and me loving you. Man to man.

Brad shows no interest in Marcos's affection. He is more excited about some talk show he had seen about adults who go through a lot of shit when they're young and how they have to "like, work it out, or else they keep doing it over and over again." Then this "cute guy" drives up in a blue convertible and Marcos tries to get in and offer a deal. Brad confides to me that no one will date Marcos now.

> **Brad:** He's too cross-eyed and ugly and dresses like trash.

Marcos returns empty handed, saying it was no go because the guy doesn't like black girls.

Plummer Park

Black Anthony points at my face and promises that he will never get old. He was a kid not so long ago. Now he's very drunk, bloated, scarcely supporting a cheap wine habit.

The Boulevard

When she sees me, Blade gets down on her knees on top of the Marilyn Monroe star in front of Hollywood Mickey D's. She is begging for money and for me to sign some papers for a van that she and Tank want to buy. So far they've saved $4. Tank is drunk. They want to drive up to her dad's and impress him with the van, then get married in Reno. This way they'll have a reason to stay out of jail. Tank sings:

> *"They grow us big, they grow us strong,*
>
> *living for combat to right their wrongs.*
>
> *For we are the future, it's all up to us,*
>
> *us and the battle lord, it's us to bust.*
>
> *Warchild, born to take lives,*
>
> *Warchild, forced to fight, crash, and burn."*

Across the Boulevard, Wea, Macki, and a new girl, Universe, have cornered some trendy teenagers from the suburbs. Wea is demanding that they give up their boots. One girl whines.

> **Girl:** It's not fair.
>
> **Universe:** Fuck fair. We are the streets. What's yours is mine, what's mine is yours, and I don't have nothing.
>
> **Wea:** After two weeks out here I don't even remember why I ran away. I do know that we're a long way from the mall and I need some new boots.

Wea's parents wanted her to be a good little girl, to dress proper, be a fashion designer. Everything was planned for her. Then she turned 10 and decided to grow up, rebel, and follow the rainbow. For her there is no going back.

The Valley parents arrive to pick up their frightened Valley children.

Sunday, 8:00 a.m., Plummer Park

Across the way, ten sheriffs are busting someone. Rodney bums a cig from me, watching. Pointing to his pants, metal-edged dick. Loaded. No safety. Hubba rattling in his unfolded hand.

> **Rodney:** They're looking for guns but those stupid fucks can't find nothin'.

FUCK ITS ABOUT FUCK THE NICITIES IN LIFE

FUCK WASHING CLOTHES AND SHOWERS AND

ALL THAT SHIT

9:00 a.m.

At Flynn squat I find Darby asleep in a bush. Hippie Dave is living in a box, trying to slam a crushed Valium pill in his arm with a blunted point. He keeps missing his veins so he gets red bumps. We climb up the hill and eat the Nutter Butters that Hippie Dave found in the trash. At the camp are Tweeky Dave, Ziggy, Tartak, Freckie, and Perry. They are all going crazy over Jersey Lu and Kristy, two very cute, freshly arrived girls from New Jersey. Their bags have broken zippers and are filled with lots of clothes, a hairdryer, numerous "Seventeen" magazines, a hairbrush, rubber bands for braces, make-up, contact lens solution, and birth control pills. A radio blasts AM music and a pink dress hangs from a tree.

Jersey Lu: You guys shoulda been here last night. It was a trip. We just got all our luggage up here and we were like chillin' and Kristy goes "Oh, there's a cop."

Kristy: And I kept sneezin' and sneezin' and sneezin'. And Perry gets all aggro on me and starts shushing me. But we didn't get caught. We moved back here about two a.m. or so, and ended up talking all night.

Dave: It was purely intellectual. She had me snortin' mousse.

Jersey Lu: It was kinda fun. I discovered somethin' neat. Guys think they look like shit and girls don't think they do. And then girls think they look like shit and guys don't think they do.

Perry: Too bad. I slept like a pig. Had a dream I was married to a blow dryer. I woke up and thought I was blowing people I didn't know.

Dave: The whole soundtrack to my dream last night was Aerosmith. It was pornographic.

Jersey Lu: Heavy or just light?

Dave: Pretty light. You know Aerosmith.

Kristy: What's on the agenda for today? Where's our tour guide?

Tartak: Wanna go to a movie?

Jersey Lu: You got money?

Dave: Hey listen, no problem. We can sneak in.

Jersey Lu: I don't wanna do no illegal shit.

Hippie Dave: We don't do that much illegal stuff. Rob. Steal. Borrow cars. Borrow bikes. That's all.

Perry: I have an idea. Do you wanna go to church?

Kristy: You wanna have my smelly socks in your face, Perry?

Dave: Actually, if we go to church at four o'clock we can eat. The canteen doesn't open 'til tomorrow. And I'm hungry as a motherfucker. Do you have any barbecue sauce? I'm gonna kill a lizard. I get pretty vicious when I'm hungry.

Freckie: I could do with a slice of pizza.

Dave: Change the music, man.

Kristy: This is my tune, Linda Ronstadt. They made this song for me. I used to sing this all the time in the car with my mom.

Dave: If you've been thinking about your mom so much then why are you on the streets?

Kristy: 'Cause it's fun. Yesterday we were walkin' down the Boulevard and this giant lion walked up to us. I swear, I could handle this for another week or so.

Dave: Go home now.

Freckie: Fuck that home shit. We're gettin' this apartment and for the next five months our goal is to get really fat and do drugs and be lazy. I wanna go to AA and go, "I'm a drug addict and an alcoholic. And I'm downer than down." Take a big bow and then light up a big fat joint.

Kristy: I'm lonely. I'm gonna get a puppy and name it Megadeth.

Freckie pulls me aside and asks for a buck so he can buy Kristy a rose so she'll feel better. I give him two.

At the parking lot church, 4:30 p.m.

Preacher: The reason we're here is that we had a real radical revelation from Jesus Christ. I can feel your pain. Be prepared.

Dave: Fuck it. I hate having to listen to some guy tell me what I already know before I can even get something to eat. I'm starving, dude. I'm goin' to panhandle, maybe try to find Echo. Get high. Maybe sleep.

Preacher: I can feel your pain. Be prepared for what might happen. If you embrace Jesus our Lord this very minute ....

Dave: Jesus never said that shit. He said, "Feed 'em and clothe 'em." Let's go.

Back at my hotel I see four guys through the window, standing naked, switching TV channels, and drinking beer. A whore sits with her door open, drapes drawn, legs spread, bath robe apart, while across Hollywood Boulevard the street is blocked off and limousines arrive, one after another, delivering stars to the world premiere of "Robocop." As a publicity stunt, the "policeman of the future" flies through the air, up and down the Boulevard, with a jet-powered backpack. He sails past my window like a hallucination that comes from being sleep-deprived, complete with thunderous claps and action-adventure music. Then the street is open again and everything is back to normal. I try to sleep.

Several ways to fuck with cops

Confuse them
Flip 'em off
Poke holes in their tires

I called my parent's a year ago and they
said good luck and have a nice life· and that's all
just dont' come home

Burger King

Dave: You're fuckin' up, man. Don't be an asshole. If I was doing something on people who lived in houses, I wouldn't say they were all the same. Would you? You can't say that about street kids. You can't take me, Cookie, Ziggy, and Freckie, and lump us together. The streets are like rock and roll: short, fast, and hard. James Dean would have died of AIDS if he were still alive. This is not a round trip ticket. There's no goin' back. My life story would make a million bucks if it were a film. The street is my TV set. I can take a hit of acid or a shot of speed while a fuckin' normal 16 year old hangs out in a mall smoking Marlboros. Fuck if I know wh...."

Bon Jovi runs in, panting.

Bon Jovi: Someone fucking robbed me, man. Fucking Frank stole all my shit, man. Fuck. I'll never trust a motherfucker out here again. Fuck, he better be on the fucking highway, man. You gotta cigarette?

He leaves as fast as he had arrived.

Dave: Just like prime time TV, man. Something always happening.

Jim: Dreams, Dave?

Dave: See the world. Fuck all the girls I wanna fuck — in a bed instead of in the dirt. Go to all the concerts I wanna go to. Write all the music I wanna write.

Vyper comes in while we're making a list of our favorite musicians.

Vyper: I just got outta jail, man. They were telling me I had felonies and shit. I was in for kidnapping and being under the influence. I was in there planning out my whole life and I decided that I'm going into a drug rehab program. And then the motherfuckers let me out. Shit.

Dave: Yeah, and I'm going into a tweek program. Free dope. Gimme a marker, Jim. I can feel a song comin' on.

A pregnant Rag Doll cruises by searching for a TV crew. She heard they are looking for a homeless teenager who is pregnant, and they are willing to pay.

Rag Doll: People are nice to me now that I'm going to have a baby. Treat me nice and courteous. How come they weren't so nice to me before?

Dave: Yeah, where the fuck were all these film crews and photographers when I was 10 years old and really needed them?

Blade walks in looking good. She says she is now an expensive call girl, at least until Tank gets out of jail. Blade wants me to take pictures of her so she can be a model and buy the good drugs. She is sketching hard. On the back of a place mat, the four of us list the names of all the kids we know on the street. Vyper gives Dave two feet of chain and a lock to put around Echo's neck.

I go to the free food give-out at Plummer Park. I meet Pops, the speed dealer and pimp. He says he now controls the freeway squat. He has nine girls and seven boys who work for him. He says he helps them. They have talent shows up at Errol Flynn squat. He's 36 and looks like 56, been a tweek for twenty some years and he's still alive. He carries a whip. I feel safer knowing that he knows me.

San Francisco

Marcos is back in the city, trying to pull a date while talking to me on the phone.

    Marcos: Brad stole all the rent money to get high. No one has seen him. I think he's dead. Too bad, I loved him so much. So I'm back on the street, girl.

I can hear him bend over the car door to negotiate. He hung up before the wipe of the hand across the face, when the trick said yes.

Christmas

Marcos's hotel room is too small for both the loud TV and his voice which rises with it.

    Marcos: My new daddy owns this famous café. He got me this room. He comes over and I jack him off. He comes real quick and then he goes to sleep. Easy money. I will suck him dry.

Marcos yawns as he motions up and down, hands cupped to his mouth. He daydreams about becoming a go-go dancer. Then when he becomes rich he can help everyone who needs it. He is trying to prove to me how nice and sweet and good he really is, something he was never able to do for his own family. And just as quickly, his voice turns cold as he begins thinking out loud about how much he could milk from the sugardaddy.

Sitting on a roof drinking ~~beer~~ beer

Me, Keven, and Johnny,

~~Eve Doing~~ Doing Everything our parents don't
Want us to do

Suck, ~~F~~

Fuck.

Lick

Swallow

Genocide
Hippy
Dumbo
Schemer
Shotgun
Tiny
gayboy
Cub
Cupcake
Cutey
Acid
Dead Rick
Dead Mike
~~Deadhead~~
Feather
Mohawk John
Pockets
Puppet
CRAZY ERIC
Ninja Todd
Flake
STOOPID
Cheater
Damien #2
~~Demon~~
Demon
DESIRE
DESIRÉE
Dykette
Lucifer
~~Rat~~ Toon
DIG
Q.T.
Sperm
~~Illin~~
Zipper
Tweezer
Teazer
Tiger

Pooh-Bear
CLYDE
BRUCE
THAI
BONER
SKULL
PUNK
SMOKER
SPANKY
SPANKO
REBEL
CON
KAHN
KANDI KANE
NAI TAI (Like my THAI)
DISCO DAVE
DUCK
SWANN
KIKE
LORELEI
High Pockets
RUBY
NAZI RICK
NAZI DAVE
HITLER
BRANDY
RUSH
CRUSH
OKI Dog Jimmy
OKI Dog STEVE
SHADOW (Boy + GIRL)
SCOOTER   SPICES
Ragdoll
Cerva
Witch Bitch
Candy
Runaway
Destiny
Psychette

Polk Street

Deion force-kisses me hello. Bragging 'bout the $300 he made from some porno movie, he says he will be famous. He demands that I take his picture. He demands money. He wants me to come take pictures of all of them smoking hubbas. Marcos shows up with a photo of his sugardaddy, a fat, balding, and extremely passive looking middle-aged man. Marcos says he is getting it together.

> **Marcos:** Look, I already started school but missed a week 'cause I am too stressed over some kid who died. Ian was his name. Boom. Look what the "daddy" gave me.

Marcos shakes a set of keys. A new Jeep is illegally parked across the street. I ask to see his name on the registration. He gets in the driver's seat, and as he slams the door and starts the car the power windows go down.

> **Marcos:** Don't worry, he'll give it to me.

Snap, snap. As he drives away, I see Rhonda and Jill coming out of an alley with scored rock, laughing, happy, singing, "Why shouldn't we get stupid?" before I could even ask.

A few weeks later

Marcos calls to tell me that he went through a red light and there was a bad accident. The Jeep was totaled and he might've killed a motorcyclist. The police are waiting to see if the man dies before they bring charges against him. Marcos is laying low in a hotel room that the sugardaddy got for him.

Troll squat, Hollywood

Nobody around. Too early, I guess. I find OD sleeping on cardboard in a burned-out building. His bed is moldy piss newspapers covered with shit piles and flies. He's nodding out while standing up. I hear voices in the back. Kids doing drugs. Out of the dark comes a wigged-out mid-20s skin.

>**Manson:** My name is Manson. I just got out of jail. There, all I wanted was dope, every fucking day for three years. That's 2,095 days, man. All I thought about that whole time was getting high. Now that I'm out, all I can think about is quitting tomorrow.

Manson gives me a dollar to take care of Darby.

>**Manson:** Don't want him to end up like me, man.

Back at Flynn squat a power struggle is evolving. Psycho puts out cigs on his body, then sticks safety pins through his skin. Wea is licking Psycho's wounds. Psycho and Riff Raff have taken over the camp. No one wants to argue with Psycho.

For my 12th B-DAY, MY OLD MAN Grabbed me and gave me a carton of smokes and a sheet of acid. Looking back now I would have rather gotten a hug but the only time my father would put his hands on me would be to beat the shit out of me.

The next day I went to school and dropped 5 hits in my teacher's coffee when she had turned her back. Few minutes later she started writing all stranger shapes and figures on the board and passed out. The nut was out for a week.

I WANT TO GET MARRIED AND HAVE
AT LEAST FOUR KIDS WITH 10 DOGS,
AND LIVE IN A MANSION WITH A JUNGLE
GREENHOUSE WITH A PET JAGUAR.

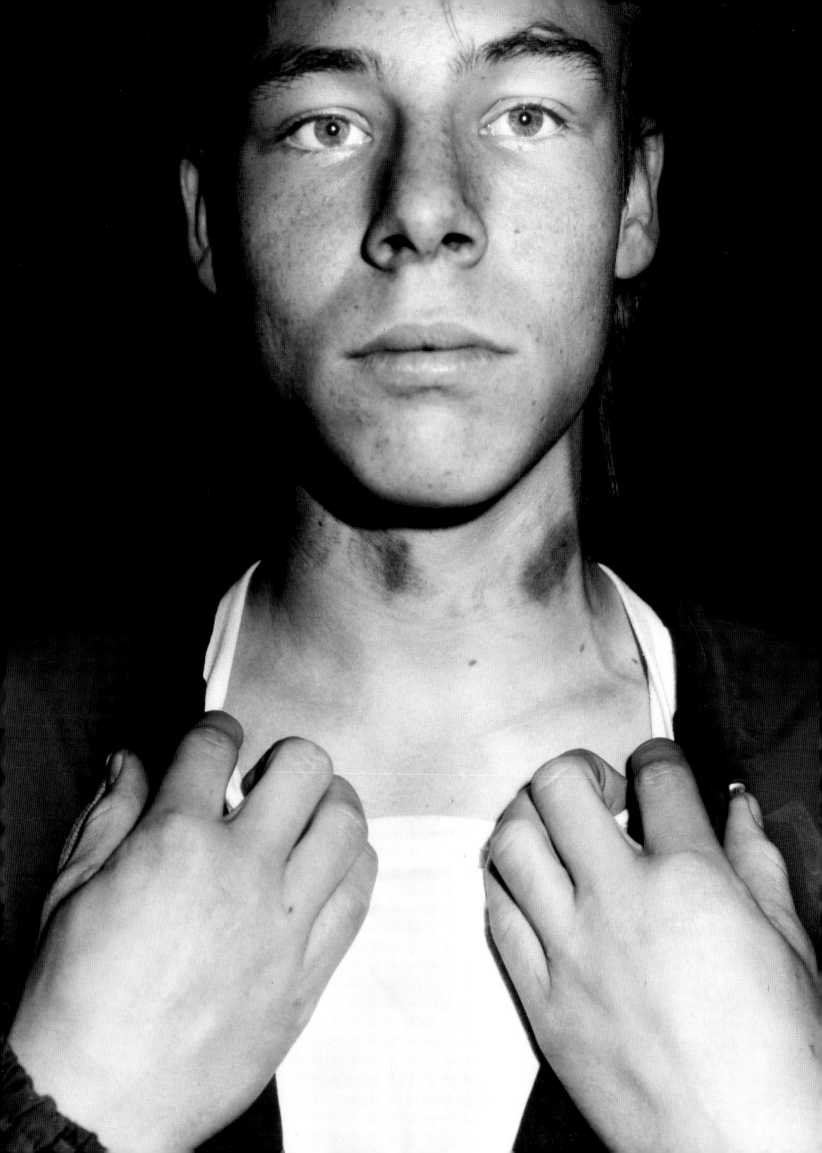

When I turn 18 I'm going in the marine corp
my DAD WAS in the ~~marine~~ marines
He DieD in veitnam

I want to Be like my DAD

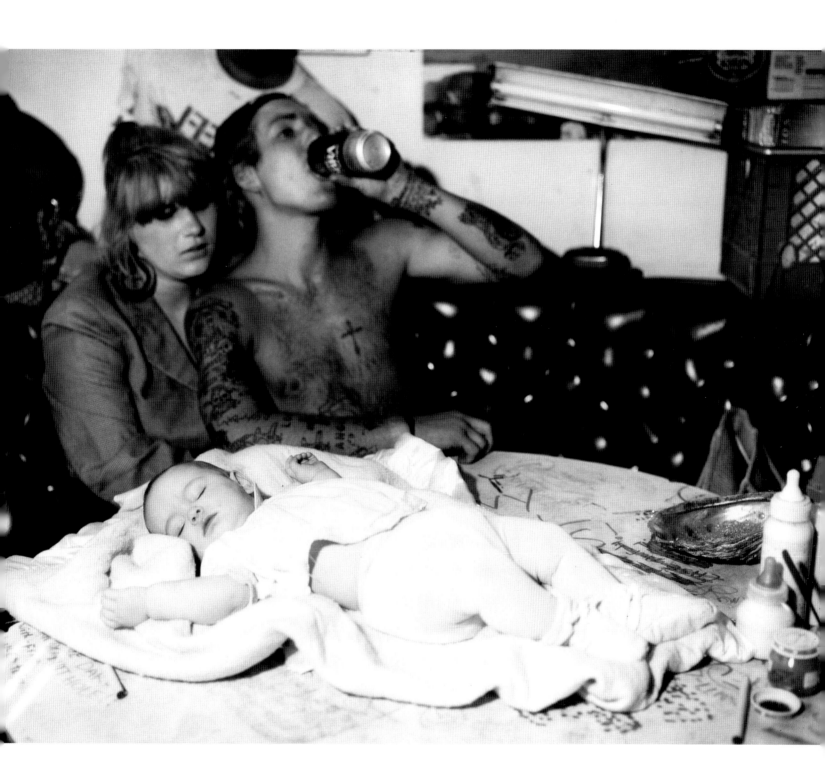

Next Fall

Echo is not at Teen Canteen.

Dave: I broke up with her but I'm still a junkie for her, man.

Jim: What do you mean? This sounds serious.

Dave: Do you understand what I'm saying? Logically speaking, I'm dying of leukemia and I shouldn't even be bothered about having a girlfriend. Like, if you're gonna die, you don't wanna fuck your life up with a girlfriend, 'cause you could get hurt. But then again, if you're dying, you're hurting anyway. And who the fuck wants to hurt alone? So what the fuck do you do? I'll tell you a secret, Jim. She's a bag-chasing whore who doesn't fuck. She's a yuppie reject runaway who couldn't handle that routine. Usually when these kids ain't into sex it's because somethin' bad happened to them a while ago.

Plummer Park. No Echo. Ziggy comes dragging out of the bushes.

Ziggy: I heard that Echo was hanging in Greco's Pizza on Sunset with some tweeker pimp from hell, a real loser. And if you see Cookie, tell her I love her.

We find Echo on Hollywood Boulevard. She is watching a drunk on a bench taunt kids with $100 bills. Echo, Dave, and I cruise the Boulevard, window-shopping for teenage things to buy. Dave gets down on his knees on top of Rudy Vallee's star. He proposes to Echo. He stands on a bus bench and begs her to fuck him. She'd rather have a t-shirt or get high. We go to Sunset Denny's. Surrounded by long-haired-rich-kid-rock-and-roll-in-purposely-torn-Spandex-pants-types who dress like they want to live on the street, Echo orders two banana splits and a Chocolate Hot Fudge Cake Sundae. Dave orders oatmeal and puts fifteen packets of sugar into the bowl. Echo's new boyfriend, Axel, shows up and tries to pimp a young girl to me. Axel threatens Tweeky Dave and swears he will kill him, then leaves. Echo sobs, realizing that her boyfriend is a "psycho pimp" and she doesn't know how to get out from underneath him. Dave hugs her and speaks of hope. They decide to go together on a drug mission. I drop them off at Oki Dogs.

November 3, night, Hollywood

I walk the Boulevard, back and forth. Then back again. Dave comes out from the shadows of the Oasis alley. Now he has a mohawk.

Dave: I'm looking for love, or Echo, or whatever comes first. I want to get back to my punk roots.

Dave starts singing, "I did it my way...," improvising lines about Echo dying with him. He is with Cookie and Ziggy, who are now engaged to each other. Cookie says she is pregnant. They had just scammed enough money for a hotel room and chips, sodas, and cigs from a TV crew. At the Hollywood Palms Motel, Cookie asks for room 23. They like that room with its TV and big bed. Cookie and Ziggy find some of their old tags.

Dave says he's even thinking of taking a shower. Cookie is cock-teasing the boys with nothing on but a towel. There is a party feel to it, until they want to get high. By the time Baby Face arrives they can think of nothing else. He has two beepers and six ounces of 151 Bacardi rum, not enough to get them drunk. So they decide to shoot up ten cc's of rum mixed with ten cc's of water — each. Cookie and Baby Face want more. She and Ziggy argue. Ziggy doesn't think it's a good idea for Cookie to do more, since she's pregnant. He thinks that he should do it. Dave wants them all to shut the fuck up so he can go to sleep in the closet. At 1:30 a.m., Baby Face and Cookie leave to try to sell the beepers and buy a gram of speed. Ziggy starts crying. Dave crawls into the bed to hug him to sleep, both knowing that Cookie wouldn't be back before check-out time.

Preacher Hilton

Jim: Okay, so, about Dave?

Hilton: So, uh, David is just kind of a heartbreak case. I've heard him tell me that he has AIDS. That might be a confidential statement. Also, he says that he has leukemia and that he was addicted to heroin when he was born. And then David has a massive scar on his stomach. He says that he walked in on his father doing a drug deal and that his own father shot him. He comes to church services about every Sunday. And he has a relationship with God, in his own way.

Let's see, David is what I call a chronic kind of street person. I don't think he will make it off of the street because he has such a psychological addiction to that life. So, what he needs is a family there to be a positive influence on him, like a big brother.

These kids find their greatest human need, which is the need for love and affection, met out on the streets with a peer group that will love and accept them. They become greater than a family. You know, they would rather live in filth and hunger with a group that will accept them than they would with a family that will meet all their physical needs, yet inflict on them emotional pain and torment.

Officer Ruby, L.A.P.D.

Jim: Why are these kids on the street?

Officer Ruby: Child abuse and discipline. Kids just aren't disciplined enough to do what they're supposed to. They don't know what responsibility is today and they're the future of America. It all has to do with discipline and most of these kids come from families where everything's given to them. Usually I drop a kid off and they're back in Hollywood before I am. The system is screwed up. The programs don't work. State's payin' for it.

Jim: What do most police officers think about the kids?

Officer Ruby: Policemen don't like to mess with the kids 'cause they're a hassle to deal with. You know, more paperwork, more of a burden to law enforcement.

Jim: Tweeky Dave?

Officer Ruby: People go to Dave for advice and all that. I met Dave six years ago. Dave's gonna die on the streets. We verified he has leukemia. He wants to die around the people he knows. All I know for a fact is that his dad shot him. I've never seen a bullet wound like that. It's a very messy scar. He told me he is 26. He told me his real name is Bruce Miller and that he's never been arrested. He panhandles to buy just enough drugs to use them.

Jim: You think Dave's a bad kid?

Officer Ruby: When it comes to survival, I know Dave does what he has to do. He's surviving. It may be bad what he's doin', but he's doin' what he has to do. I know Dave has done bad things, but I don't consider him a criminal.

Jim: How is Dave different from other kids?

Officer Ruby: I think he has words of wisdom. The kids go to him first. They go to him for guidance. He's outside of all the coolness, outside of the violence. Yeah, he really cares, especially about Echo. Her mom came out here. She offered to put 'em both up in an apartment. They didn't wanna go.

These kids come out here with a dream that'll never come true. They might be a walk-on or an extra in a movie, but that's all. You get all these fake producers. Maybe they're porno producers but they exploit the kids. Maybe they'll take 'em in or help 'em out and then they'll go, "Hey! I helped you out and now you're gonna go on the streets and make me some money." Hollywood preys on 'em. It's fun for maybe a year. Like Rag Doll. I met her when she first came out here. Looked like a normal person. Six months later, shaved head and skinny, ugly. If you don't catch these kids within a week or two, they're lost to a family they didn't even have at home.

Mindy Lennon, youth counselor

Jim: What do you think about Dave?

Mindy: Why isn't he dead? Why doesn't he have AIDS like all his friends? I've set up doctors appointments but Dave never follows through. He is afraid of confronting his mortality. He is the only client to take the worst clothes here. He's the most scarred person. The doctors say, "One more needle and he'll be dead." They are trying to scare him. I know he's had that one more needle and he's still alive. Dr. Cohen saw him when he had hepatitis. He looked at him and said to himself, "Why isn't Dave dead? This child should not be alive." The doctors also say that he doesn't have leukemia. That it's something else. He says he's 19. No one even knows. I don't know why he isn't dead, maybe he's lucky. Certainly his physical self is dead. Before the streets, drugs, IV use, and hustling — medically — his body is not right.

I don't relate much to the idea of a god, but with Dave, he really wants to help people. It's as if he is obsessed, angelic. Dave is very humanistic. He seems to be on a mission to help the homeless. So there is some will to live in him, to pass on his knowledge and good nature. It's a mystery. Dave is an inspiration to people. He is society's throw-away.

Cop

A police car radio buzzes in the background.

Cop: There's so much paperwork in this town.

Jim: Do you know Tweeky Dave?

Cop: Yeah, we just arrested him.

Jim: What was Dave like when you arrested him?

Cop: He's terrible. He can't experience pain. He's got no place to hit, he's all bone, he's beat up.

C'mere, c'mere, c'mere. Put your hands on the car. Put your hands in the air. Step out in the middle of the street, put your hands on your head. Step out in the middle of the street or I'll blow your fuckin' head off.

Tweeky Dave's opinion about these people

Jim: How do most cops treat you, Dave?

Dave: Less than shit.

Jim: What are cops usually like?

Dave: Rednecks with hard-ons. They got beat up when they were in school so now they wanna prove they're bad. Closet case homosexuals.

Jim: What about Preacher Hilton?

Dave: I don't get along with him religiously. My views on religion change day to day. I have a lot of respect for him 'cause he'll help people. Dude's given me his last dollar. He's fed me when he even didn't have something to eat himself. He doesn't look at us like we're any different from him. He looks at us like we're people.

Jim: Are adults hypocrites?

Dave: Some. Some street people are hypocrites. You can't say this group or that group are hypocrites. Some photographers are hypocrites.

Jim: What about youth service programs?

Dave: Most of the programs, I think, are basically trying but they ain't doing shit. Dude, there's fifty beds for a thousand kids.

Jim: What about all the rules?

Dave: The rules suck, man. People shouldn't be concerned with what color my hair is or what length it is or what my t-shirt says. They should care about if this kid is hungry or not. Does this kid need a bath? Does this kid need a place to sleep?

Jim: Why don't programs work?

Dave: Because, dude, they come down too hard. The rules are too extreme, man. I mean, they say they've gotta change the street kids' lives. Well, that's true. But you can't take somebody from point A to point Z overnight. You can't make me a fuckin' suburban teenager now, after what's gone down. It'll never happen. My whole attitude, my whole bearing, is fuckin' different than the attitude of people in the suburbs.

Jim: Why do you think that is?

Dave: 'Cause of what I've had to do to survive. When you've had to suck dick and eat out of dumpsters, it's a little different than if you could just walk up and say, "I'm hungry, mom." It's hard to follow a law when you've gotta eat. You're gonna dumpster-dive. You're gonna panhandle. You're gonna sell your body. It's hard to follow a program when you don't believe in anything. It's hard to believe in God if you don't believe in anything. There's my answer. See, all these things I'm supposed to believe in — God, the police, the programs — I don't believe in them. Shit, man, what I really believe is that I'm gonna walk and go buy a book 'cause I got three dollars in my pocket. We are the black sheep of the American family. Quit looking for an answer, Jim. There fuckin' ain't one. Fuck yeah, I'm still looking for God's telephone number.

From ~~go~~ ~~gE~~ oRgiA to ARizoNA
to L.A. then to SeAttle
to tAcomA to Fresno then to Here (S.F.)

I wAnt to go to
Port lAnD

Springtime, Hollywood

Lollipop sucking street kids hustle in drag. Ziggy is riding up and down, scoping for someone who might use his bike for a day in exchange for a quarter gram of speed. Drunk Steve says he drank forty five kegs of beer. Red Man silently walks by in tweek mode. He has a death scythe in his hand. Doc's in jail for the rest of his life. I hear (again) that Tweeky Dave's got a month to live, that he's so skinny he only weighs ninety pounds, that he's coughing up blood, and that Echo is in trouble, killing herself with whoring and drugs.

June 3, Paradise Hotel, San Francisco

The door is kicked in at Rhonda and Jill's. Hubba. There are other girls staying there, all whores tricking for rocks. Jill has a black eye. Apparently Rhonda is paranoid and is beating up on her. Crystal says she just had a seizure from smoking too much crack. They are all bored. Dirty clothes and empty pizza boxes are spilling out of the closet. They say the sheriff is coming tomorrow to kick them out. They don't care.

Polk Street

Deion "borrows" a car. It's full of excited kids, loudly listening to AM radio and looking for hubba.

> **Deion:** I got seven sugardaddies and, Miss Thang, I'm gonna be rich. I got $1,100 in my pockets right now.

Deion drives from one shithole to the next with no apparent luck. I follow, lose him, and then find him again, his car broken down at a dreadful place in Potrero Projects. The car is surrounded, a gun pointing at Deion's head. Kids flee the scene, asking me for a ride. Then some money is passed, rocks. Everything's cool. Back at the motel, it's me, Marcos, Deion, Jill, Rhonda, and Damien. In walks the sugardaddy with a box of cheap lighters. Everyone is happy and they fight over which color lighter they'll get. Marcos confides to everyone that the sugardaddy smokes crack to lose weight. Laughter. The sugardaddy looks like he might not know how to speak.

The doors and windows are sealed with towels. They set up. Gloves — smoke — flames. Everyone is quiet. (No joy.) The smoke alarm keeps going off. Soon, Rhonda is begging Marcos for more. Jill whines for a piece of rock Deion has hidden in his shoe. Damien is rolling on the floor, semi-conscious. Marcos is hitting the sugardaddy.

Dazed, I watch a sitcom on their TV about a young, poor girl adopted by an older, rich man. He offers her anything. The girl says she doesn't want to be rich. She just wants to go home to be with her real dad. "There are plenty of kids without parents. Please go take care of them," she says. And I am with these kids who aren't TV documentary cute.

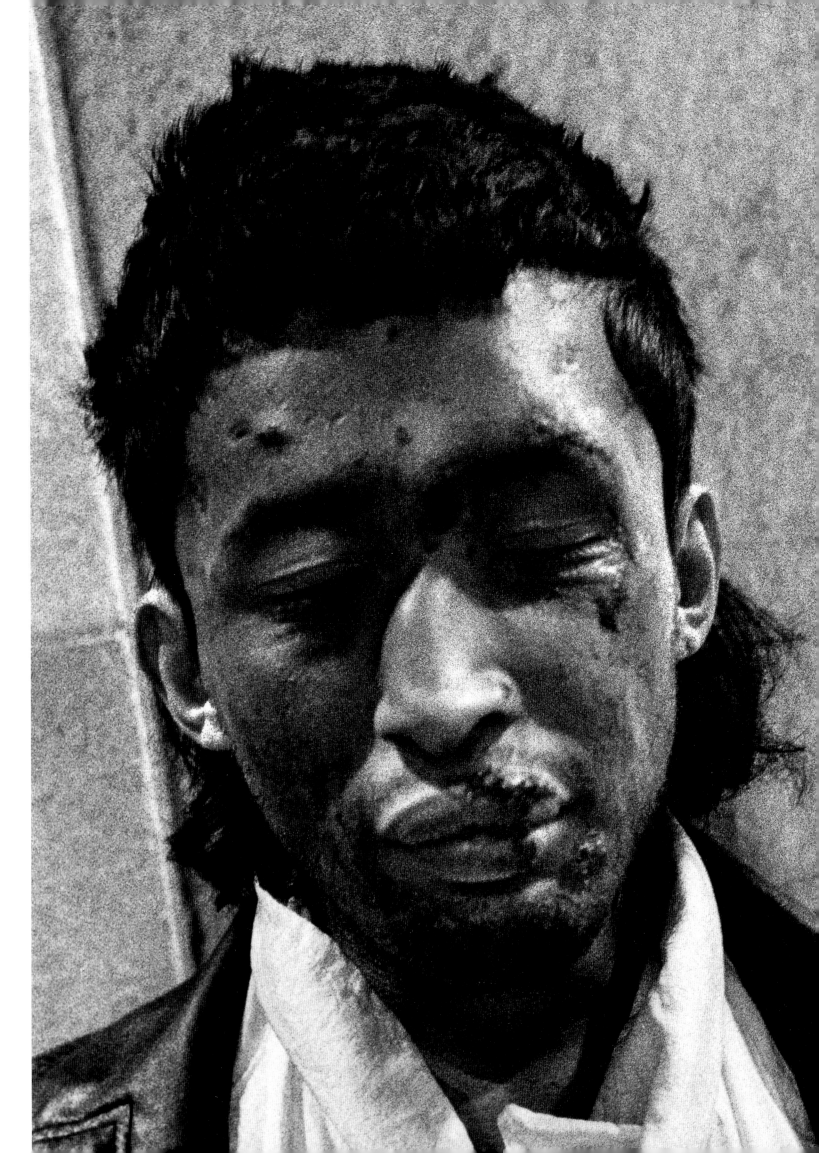

Their dimples are fading, replaced by sores. The people in this room don't recognize me any more.

July, Polk Street

Desperation is setting in all around. At two a.m., Deion is extremely stoned, promising me anything, begging me for money for hubba. He threatens me when I refuse. He tries to snap his fingers but there is no contact. I find Marcos and the sugardaddy barricaded in their room at the Marina Hotel. Both are pale and can barely communicate.

> **Jim:** Marcos, how much are you smoking?
>
> **Marcos:** I'm addicted.
>
> **Sugardaddy:** Shssssh, don't be so negative.

Late July

Marcos calls at three a.m. He moved into an apartment in San Diego with Brad, paid for by the sugardaddy. I was their first phone call.

> **Marcos:** I have pots and pans, food in the fridge, a bed, and so many clothes in my closet the bar holding them is gonna bust. Brad is with me. I am in love. No more hubbas. I decided I'm a born alcoholic, and right now, child, I'm on a natural high. I feel that I can do anything. I'm gonna get me a job and go to school and....

He mumbles something about the clap.

> **Marcos:** You know, child, at least I ain't like that girl, Angel. She died of AIDS.

One week later

> **Marcos:** I thought I would be happy down here. I'm depressed. Brad has blown me away for some guy who sells pot. Everyone always leaves me. I can't go back to the sugardaddy. What am I gonna do?

Saturday

Blade calls from a pay phone up north. She wants me to come get her. She's depressed. Tank is lost in a dumpster somewhere in Hollywood.

> **Blade:** I had to get out of it, that high-class hooker life, the dope, that relationship. I'm at my biker dad's and I'm scared. I think I remind him of my mom. Last night we took acid. He hugged me and rocked me to sleep. I woke up this morning and he was jerking off on my back.

Tuesday, Golden Gate Park

> **Jim:** What about your dad? Do you want to talk about it?
>
> **Blade:** I'd rather talk about drugs. I need some uppers.

Beaver: Someone stole my Thorazine. All I got is this American Express card.

Blade: Let's go to New York. We could fuckin' go to Europe.

Monique: I need to go shopping.

Beaver: My mom is set, she's a broker at Prudential. She told me to use this card only if I really needed it. And I say now is as good a time as any. I can see her when she gets the bill. She'd be running into her bathroom, downing her Valiums, screaming, "Denise is at it again. I tried so hard with her. Where did I go wrong? I did not raise my daughter to be called a Beaver." Blah, blah, blah. She's really fuckin' sprung. She's probably still saying it's all my fault. Well fuck her.

Blade: I need some more drugs.

Monique: I need a boyfriend, man. I haven't had sex in five months. I'm a virgin again.

Blade: I haven't had sex in four days.

Monique: After a month you're a virgin again. It grows back.

Blade: Don't be stupid. Who told you that?

Monique: A doctor said so.

Beaver: I want to go to a disco.

Blade: I saw Johnny Rotten at The Scream. And afterward, you know, I was like going to see him. I walked into his hotel room and he was in there with two chicks and fuckin' needles everywhere. It was a gnarly scene.

Night

Susan and I are parking our car at Waller and Divisadero. It's late. We hear something on the corner. A girl's head is in her arms, she's crying on the curb.

Jim: Are you okay?

Everything she says is crazy "blue electric death" talk. The girl keeps saying that she's sorry, that she is the problem. We bring her home and make her some tea. The girl is high on ten hits of acid and very suicidal. We try, but can't talk her down. I make some phone calls to find out where to get help, explaining the situation over and over. We are finally told to go to the hospital. We are in the waiting room for two hours, and all this time she is laughing and crying. Eventually, a burned out doctor shows up. He sees her in between bites of meat loaf and mashed potatoes.

Doctor: Everything's normal. Seems like she'll be okay.

Us: WHAT?

Doctor: What else can I do? No beds or staff. And with all the cutbacks....

The girl is still laughing and crying.

Us: What can we do?

Doctor: Take her to the crisis clinic.

I wanna get a car → drive to New York but I sorta don't know how to drive

It's four a.m. We can scarcely contain the girl in the three blocks between the hospital and the modular clinic. She's not crying now, but she says her socks are the devil. I give her cigs. She hands me a slip of paper.

Girl: This guy will know how to find me. He is on a psychology trip. He makes me have sex all the time.

An uncaring intake worker starts to take her away.

Girl: And I hate sex!

Fame Café, Hollywood

Vyper: I go to a luxury apartment. I take my knife and pry the door open. I walk in, take the elevator down to the garage, walk around quietly, scoping out the place, making sure there's no one there to see me. I look for an escape route. I find a car that has the most stuff in it. Then I press the button on a stopwatch to time myself. It should take me exactly 2.4 seconds to take a screwdriver out and break the window and get into the car. Then twenty-six seconds to take out the property. Eighteen seconds to put all the shit in a bag. Once I'm done with one car, I move on to the next. In one night I can hit about six or seven buildings. It depends on the timing. Once I'm done I bring it all to the fence. I have maybe $1,000 worth of merchandise. He gives me $100. I get me a room, cop some dope, some food, yeah, blow the money real fast. I'm so damn good I still haven't got caught.

Two days later, Hollywood Boulevard

Echo: Dave's on five hits of acid. I'm on two.

Dave: No wonder the whole city's freaking out. It's one big lake. All the hippies are swimming. I'm going to give you the yin/yang test. Ready, Echo? Are you yin or yang?

Echo: I'm soft and slow.

Dave: I must be yang, I'm hard and fast.

Echo: Sure, Dave.

Dave: Listen, Echo. I don't care about anybody but you. I'll support you for the rest of your life — that is if you can live offa $2 a day.

Echo: We'll panhandle every day.

Dave: In front of Saks Fifth Avenue. I'll buy you beer. I'll ask everybody that walks by for a penny to buy you beer.

Echo: We could make a lot of money like that.

Dave: Jim, dude, don't give her strawberries with her beer. It's ugly.

Echo: Sick! Don't get sentimental on me, asshole.

Dave: Baby, I love you so much I would drink your blood.

Echo: Don't you take anything seriously, Dave?

Dave: I take Johnny Thunder quite seriously. I take the Rolling Stones seriously. I take God seriously. I take not taking baths seriously. And I especially take drugs seriously.

Echo: Uh huh. Right on.

Later, I'm taking pictures of tweeks and stoners outside of the 7-Eleven. All of a sudden the cops pull up and shake us down.

Cop: Hands behind your back, shut up, legs spread.

I keep turning around. A cop keeps jamming his baton into my balls, saying he wants to ram my head through a plate glass window. We stand this way for maybe twenty minutes. They separate us and ask conflicting questions, trying to catch us in a lie. Then I am allowed to explain what I am doing.

Cop: Why waste your time with these kids, picture man?

McDonald's, Hollywood and Highland

Tank has cigarette burns up and down his left arm. He's dreaming.

Tank: I'd rather hurt on the outside than on the inside. I wanna go to Santa Cruz. I can get some of the best LSD there. The first fifty hits are free. This guy makes the shit. Gives me fifty hits. I drop thirteen and the dude tells me, "You've got to know, to dare, to do, to be silent." And I have the most wonderful trip. I go to the ocean, by the boardwalk, and it's so beautiful. You know how the waves come in? Sea gulls, palm trees, I'm trippin' man. I go up a level. I have so many deep thoughts. You know, I can get that same acid for sixty cents a hit and I can sell it for four bucks. Guaranteed income. In a week I'll have a solid $1,000 in the bank.

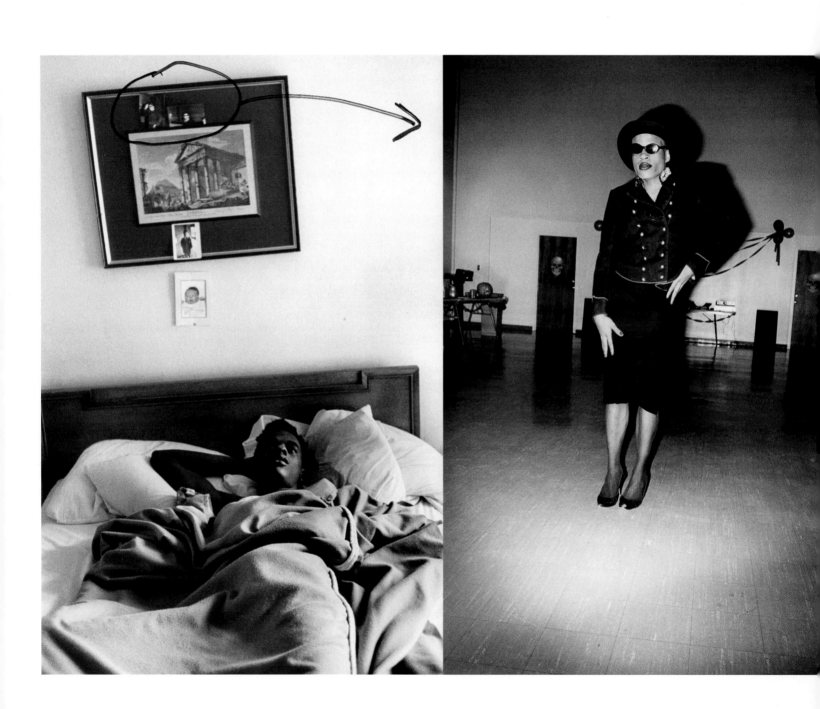

~~#~~ # WANNA PISS ON the MOON

~~PISS~~ PUT quATers in the JukeBox

AND BITCHABOUT the MUSiC

The same ol' story, Romulus and Remus, Griffith Park, LA

Due to some screw up, Colleen thinks Echo stole her clothes. Colleen told Nikki Pain, who told Cutter, that when she finds Echo she'll kill her. Dave heard all this from Patty (Colleen's best friend) and Patty told Dave that she would back up Colleen and do Echo worse than the last time, when she tore out Echo's ear lobe. Dave is scared. He knows that if any of these assholes are involved, they might make good on their promises. So he and Echo are laying low, squatting up in the hills. Echo is jonesin' from the drug profits she shot up her arms four days ago. She hasn't slept since and wants to get high so she can think this situation through. Dave is still buzzed off an eighth he got from Cookie in a trade for his radio. He knows that Echo needs to sleep and they should hide out at least until morning, long enough for both those psycho bitches to chill. Then they can be paid-off with money he'd scam. Dave tries to slip his arm under and around Echo's shoulders to comfort her. Echo is irritated. It's been like this for hours.

Echo: Dave, you're just like my pain-in-the-ass little brother.

Dave: Does your little brother want to fuck you like I do?

Echo: Dave!

Dave: Answer bitch! Is your new boyfriend Cutter ever goin' to love you like I would? Baby, all I want to do is hug you so you stay warm.

Echo: Shut up, Dave. I came here to get away from that asshole. I don't want to think about him or Colleen or anybody else right now. And I don't want to fuck you. I just want to get high. Don't you understand?

Dave: Echo, you shhhhut the fuck up! Of course I understand. I'm here to protect you, girl. Just let me tell you a bed-time story about when I first came out here and met the finest connect who had the best drugs I ever did.

Echo: Dave, I don't want to lie in your arms. And I don't want to hear some bullshit story I've heard before. I want to get high. That's all I want, just a little buzz. Nah, I'm going back to the Boulie. At least I can find me a Valium and crawl up on some fire escape to sleep, sleep, sleep....

She mumbles into a rambling bitch about killing Dave if he doesn't stop bothering her.

Echo: What difference would it make if I go back to the Boulevard? This life is all some weird dream that I'll never wake up from and I'll never, ever be normal again. I'm just going to die anyway....

Dave wishes he had a Valium or a bottle of whiskey, but he doesn't. He tries to hug her again. She tries to kick him in his balls, but misses.

Dave: Just chill, Echo. You know what will happen if you go back out there. Between Colleen and Patty and the cops, you'd be in real trouble. Shit, I've seen plenty of gorgeous chicks like you get fucked-up in the face just 'cause some

maniac junkie whore decided to smash them. No, you're too pretty to me.
Stay here where you're safe. You gots to be patient, Echo. At least 'til morning.
Then, I'll go back and panhandle us enough for a hotel room and to pay back
Colleen. Lie down and let me tell you this story I done never told anyone. And when
I'm finished we can go back to the street. No shit.

Echo: Fuck you, prick. No one ever keeps their promises. Why should I believe you
when I don't believe in anything?

She lies back down and turns away.

Dave: Listen. All that shit I said about Texas, my folks, the scar, leukemia,
the junk, it's all made up. Here's the truth. I just appeared one day in an alley off
La Brea. That's where Lupé, this wild chick, found me. She was on a tweek with
the rest of her crew and there I was, screamin' my brains out, wrapped in a bloody
blanket, bleeding at the stomach. She didn't know me from shit, but she took me
in her arms and I didn't come down for another twelve years. Me and 'bout eight
others. I swear, this bitch must have been knocked-up permanent. Seemed like
there was always some kid planted on those tits of hers.

Hell, Lupé was already a granny when she scraped me up off the sidewalk.
She was around 30, 'cept she looked 50 — all weathered and shit, like she'd been
livin' on the streets so damn long. I'll tell ya, Lupé was straight-up ugly. Nice body,
though, and great tits. Which didn't hurt business any. Sucking dick, selling tweek,
stealing, snitching to the cops, dumpster diving. She did anything to put food on
the table and stay high. From when I was about 4 'til I was 7, we crashed up here
in the rocks and bushes. Called ourselves "The Pack." We had a hell of a good
squat going.

Then we split to Patterson. Lived in a van, then back up in the hills — you
know, same ol' same ol', the Man-always-after-us kind of thing. What he saw was
only a no good junkie whore with lots of wild, dirty children, shitting and
pissin' wherever they went, addicted to who knows what kind of dope from the
day they was born. The Man was damn right, girl. We spent most of our time on
tweeks. She always had special shit and she never seemed to run out. I'm talking
"hell-a-good" drugs here, clean and even. Not like this cut up shit Nikki Pain sells,
which gets you so indicated that you're arguing about who should get high first.
No, I've seen people kill each other over bunk dope. Hell, sister, we're practically
ready to kill each other now, if you know what I mean. Echo? ECHO?

*Echo ignores him, slipping further down in her blanket, trying to get comfortable and
stay warm. Maybe even sleep. Dave doesn't care. He's buzzed enough to be very happy
listening to himself talk.*

Dave: So where was I? I remember crystal clear my first time getting high. She
came back from a long night of dates, grabbed me and her skates, and dragged
us to the park. She done set us up right there on a bench. Slammed an eighth of

a gram into me, then a quarter into her neck. And I was like, whew, rushing so bad I could feel myself lift off the ground. Fuck, I was so spun I couldn't even argue when the crazy bitch grabbed hold of my arm with her teeth and slammed me with another. By then I was dreamin' this dream that I could barely watch. She put on her skates and then ripped off her shirt. I watched her skate those perfect figure-eights. I was howling inside — I knew there was magic there, those tits risin' to the moon.

Dave hears dogs moaning in the hills up above and Echo is finally falling asleep.

Dave: For the next three days we talked all kindsa shit: about home, survival, love, and dreams. Lupé told me secrets, including the one about where I came from. It's a fuck of a story.

There was once this Hollywood politician who was a very important man. Everyone loved and respected the dude. Some people thought he could rule the whole city, maybe even the world. Just one little secret stood in his way. He had a weakness for little 12 year old girls. Lupé said she had often seen him, hunting in his big car, stopped at corners on Sunset, smooth-talkin' new trade.

Then he got this little whore pregnant and tried to buy her off to abort it, but check this out. The chick said, "fuck you and your chump-shit money, mister. I always wanted to be a mom so I could give my child everything in life that I didn't get myself." The politician couldn't risk his career over some whore's "petty" dreams of a better life. So after she was pregnant for 'round seven or eight months the sick fuck kidnapped the girl and arranged for an abortion at the hospital, 'cept there was this problem.

The doctor who was paid off to perform the operation discovered the girl was pregnant with twins — a boy and a girl. But this was no two-for-one special, so he refused to go on and the babies came anyway. The motherfuckers lived through an ugly delivery. The little girl seemed to be okay but the boy was born with only half a stomach. It was all open and bloody and shit. He shouldn't have survived but he did. A nurses' aide was paid to drown the babies. Instead, he took the money and ran. They say he gave the girl to his cousin but no one knows for sure. My sister was never found.

As for me, I was left for dead, and that's when Tweeky Lupé found me and nursed me back to health. I don't know what the bitch used to patch up my stomach. Whatever it was, it worked. The politician did okay too, making headlines for speeches about his integrity, family, democracy, and the American way. Bullshit. I was born into misery and have accepted it since. Because my daddy is a politician, I've found it's easier to tell everyone what they expect to hear: that I am a low rent, welfare number's junkie son, you know. No one would believe the truth about who I really am.

Dave looks over at Echo. She's snoring.

Dave: When I turned 12, Lupé straight-up kicked my ass out. Maybe she thought I had learned her wild ways and was ready, or maybe she just got sick of my jonesin' her for money and dope. I'm not sure, 'cause before I knew it I was curbin' it, which was cool 'cause I didn't have to wait too long for the old men to become dollar signs reflected in my eyes. That didn't last long, though, 'cause as time went by my youth faded and I got to lookin' more like my so-called ma. Haven't seen Tweeky Lupé for years. I heard she moved east with some guy, way outside of town up in the hills. That's cool — hope she's happy.

Dave rolls over on his back with only arms for a pillow.

Dave: Echo, since I love you and it looks like I can't fuck you, I can at least tell you what I think, straight-up. You need a new dream, girl, and I'm not talkin' 'bout that dumb-ass plan we have to get a hotel room and a gram. That "let's-start-worrying-about-the-future-tomorrow" type bullshit will just become permanent, I know. If that's what you're dreaming about, bitch, forget it, 'cause I don't want any part of it. Listen, the cops will always find you. And so will your sorry-ass life. Pretty soon you'll get old and scarred and look as bad as I do. Then where will you be? Girl, if you don't get out of here soon, you ain't gonna make it. Just look at me. What you need is to go home to your "Echoville" — find yourself a nice, normal, boring boyfriend, have some kids, go to the mall, and scream.

Dave puts his arm around Echo's body, kisses her, and talks to the moon the rest of the night. In the morning she is still sound asleep as Dave slips away to make good on his promise to raise some cash to buy Echo's freedom.

August 20, Sunset Boulevard

Cookie: Do you have a cigarette?

Dave: I just gave you one.

Cookie: Fuck you, dick head. I can ask you to do whatever the fuck I want to and you know it.

Dave: No, you can't do whatever the fuck you want 'cause you ain't God.

Cookie: Bullshit, Dave. I'm sick and hungry and no one's doing shit about it. Give me a cig.

Neither one is in any mood to be cute. They are both jonesin' bad. Cookie is acting like a little whore with a wicked attitude. She is on a mission to find Ziggy. Ziggy had split the night before with the dope money. She needs money for heroin and she wants new clothes — now. Dave isn't much better. He is yellow from hepatitis and coughing a lot, hasn't seen Echo or slept for a week. He thinks that hanging out with Cookie will make Echo jealous. That will then prove that she loves him and force Echo to come back to him. Meanwhile, Dave has scammed almost enough money to pay off Colleen, but Cookie and Dave's addiction is threatening to ruin it all.

Hollywood Boulevard

Echo is geeked. She now has blond hair.

Echo: Like my hair, Jim? You seen Tweeky Dave? Find him. Tell him I need him. Yesterday someone stole my Led Zeppelin jacket. And this morning, Colleen bunched me for everything I fuckin' own. She kept calling me a thief and a liar, and I kept telling her I'd pay her the money, but she was never there when I had it. You know that I never owed her in the first place. She kept aiming her knife at me and shit. And I'm like, "I'll take this up with you later, girl." So, you know how it goes. When somebody takes somethin' from you forcibly, you don't stand a rat's chance in hell of getting it back. She even ripped the lock Dave gave to me right off my neck. I'm sick of this street. It's lame. Dominos doesn't even deliver.

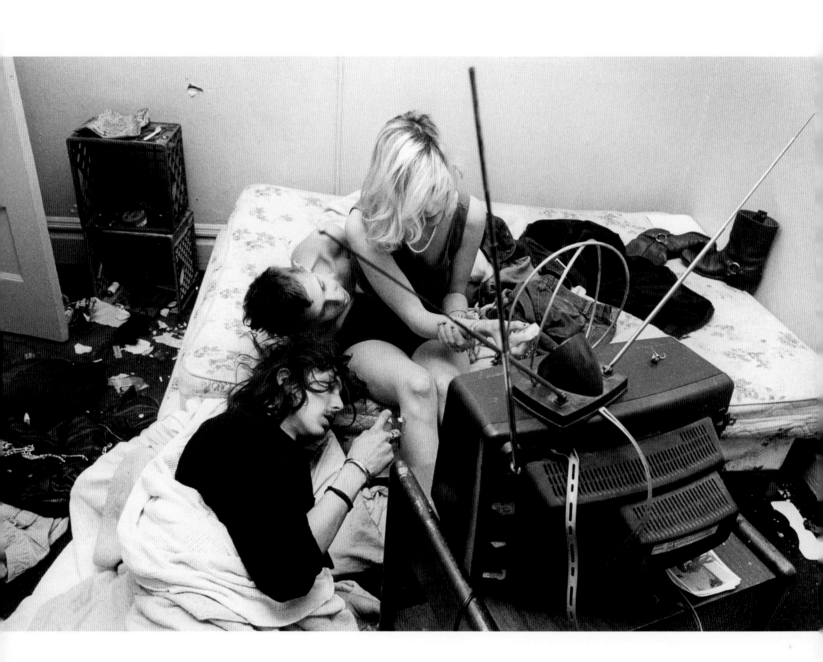

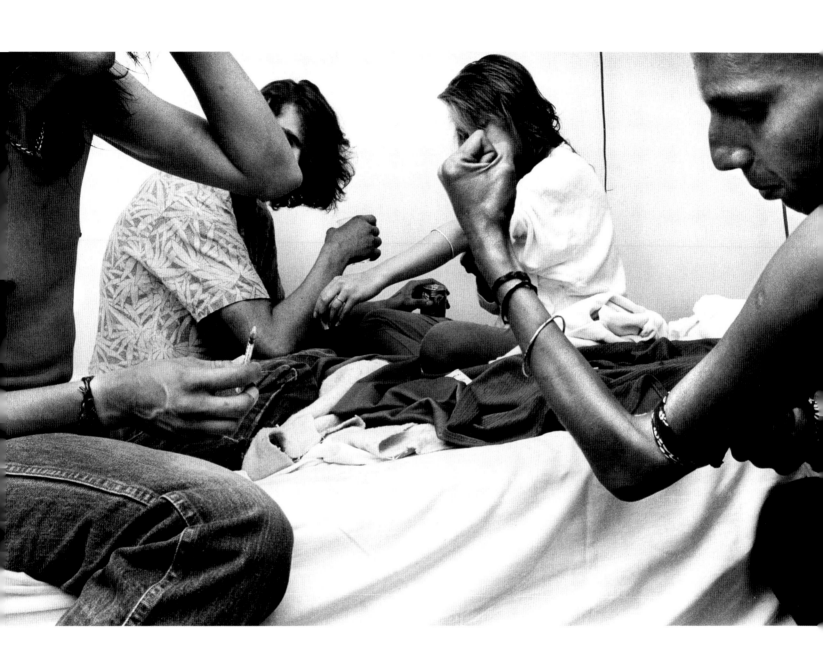

Born a wicked child
raised By wolves

A screamin kamakazi
I never will crash

Sunset Boulevard

Late summer. I buy Dave rent at Denny's. A bowl of oatmeal and a cup of coffee
costs $1.84. His lips are blistering. There is dried blood around his gums.
He's been trying to sleep off the results of his latest "life without Echo" binge.

Dave: I have hepatitis and should be in the hospital. The rumor is that I'm Jesus. And when I die they'll rename Hollywood after me. Everyone is hanging under the bridge, shootin' dope with Pops and his little girl dope fiends. Lorna is suckin' dick for money. And Blade says hi. She's doing basically the same thing I do: staying stoned for about eight months and then working for a month. Drunk Steve is still drunk. Saw him and his girlfriend two months ago. They were still out to kill each other. Rag Doll is around. She had her kid and gave it away. Freckie's down here livin' with Chance. He's workin' at a clothes store up on Melrose and drinkin' a lot. Kristy blew him off. Hear she's stripping for cocaine on mirrored glass in Florida. Jersey Lu split from Cruise 'cause he's still slammin' and she's seven months pregnant. The cops closed Oki Dogs. The Teen Shelter's bogus. You can't smoke in there. You can't sleep in there. You gotta talk to your case worker just to get something to eat. And most kids don't wanna go through all that shit just to get a peanut butter and jelly sandwich.

Jim: What's going on with Cookie?

Dave: Beat my meat to the toilet seat. Doo dah. Doo dah. Sure looks ugly but it feels real neat. Doo dah, doo dah, day. Drugs and sex. I love Cookie. She'll always be true to herself. She's straight-up nude dancin'. Perry found a magazine with a picture of her gettin' cum shot on her. She looks damn good. She said she'd fuck me if I pierced my nose.

Jim: What about Ziggy?

Dave: Cops got him for jaywalking. He's in jail for possession of cocaine. He should be out by now. Him and Echo had an off again, on again love affair for a while, 'til he told her, "Look bitch, I like dope better than I like you. And you like dope better than you like me. So get it straight."

Jim: I heard from Echo's mom that you two weren't getting along.

Dave: No, I haven't seen her in months. I wanted to stop shootin' dope, not only to make sure I still could, but for her. You know, go straight for her. Well, she couldn't handle it and got all strung out. So I said fuck it. Echo and me are two different people. I hear she's real fucked-up, hookin' way out in Palmville, livin' with her ex-sugardaddy Ian. No, me and her weren't meant for each other. I used to think we were the same but we're not. Guess I'm lookin' for a new girlfriend. Gotta go, Jim. I have an appointment.

Ian the sugardaddy

Ian decides he wants to help street kids, so he collects a bunch and brings them to his rented house out in the Valley. Calls it a "youth shelter." Every now and then he convinces someone that he's honest and they'll give him a couple hundred bucks or something and he's off on a tangent. Echo is staying there and she lives quite happily on the floor, watching TV twenty-four hours a day. I buy her a banana split at the Fame Café.

Echo: I was sitting on the wall by IHOP and I'm, like, reading a paper and Ian, like, keeps driving by going, "C'mon, just go for a ride." And I'm like, "I'm not working." And he, like, parks the car and comes up and talks to me and goes, "I don't care if you're working. I didn't say anything about working." And I go, "I'm not gonna do nothing." And he's like, "Just come for a ride." He's about 30. Glasses. A little fat, says he's into computers, and has a nice car. Well, we go to the beach and he buys me an ice cream cone and gives me his shirt when I'm cold. Says he doesn't want anything except to hang out with a pretty and smart young person like myself. And to be my friend. And to help me. He seemed nice. I went and stayed with him. He fed me. Brought me clothes. After a while he told me he didn't want to fuck me — that he liked older girls. But he told everyone else he does fuck me. So now I sort of fuck him and he sort of pays me.

FRIDAY 9-21-90 - WELL WE HAVEN'T EVEN LEFT YET & ALREADY OUR ADVENTURES
PAGE 1 BEGIN. 12:15 WE LEAVE BART FOLLOWED BY 2 BART COPS. WE SAW
THEM & PICKED UP OUR SHIT & GOT THE HELL OUT. ME, DAVE & A 6'1"
143 POUND COWBOY AQUAINTANCE OF OURS WERE CAUGHT ON THE
PARK LAWN. A NIGGER COP & A BROAD COP. DAVE HAS NO I.D. COWBOY
GIVES HIS SSI CARD & HIS REPORT COMES BACK AS A RUNAWAY.
SO THEY GOT WHAT THEY WANTED & GAVE BACK MY I.D. & LET
ME & DAVE GO. OH YEAH, WE WERE PANHANDLING. GOOD THING I
HAD ALL THE MONEY. WE MADE 5 BUCKS. WE'RE SUPPOSED TO TELL
HIS UNCLE AT C.J.'s WHAT HAPPENED BUT WE WANTED TO GET
THE HELL OUT OF TOWN BEFORE SOMETHING ELSE HAPPENED.
SO NOW WE'RE AT SAMTRANS BUS STOP WAITING TO GO. TIME!
1126 P.M. ON THE BUS & ON THE WAY! 2:24 WE'RE STILL ON
SAMTRANS IN REDWOOD CITY & THE BUS JUST PULLED IN TO GET
ITS CHANGE COLLECTED. DAVID SAT UP TO WATCH & THE BUS
DRIVER GOES "SIT UP FOOL!" WHAT A BITCH. WE HAVE EVERY
RIGHT TO BE NOSEY. WE PAID $1.50 BITCH! IT'S 2:42 & WE'RE AT
THE STANFORD MALL GOING TO PANHANDLE. 5:02 WE'RE IN
SAN JOSE NOW. WELL, ABOUT 10 MINUTES PANHANDLING. WE GOT
ENOUGH FOR THE BUS. SOME DUDE GAVE US A PACK OF CIGARETTES
& GUESS WHAT? IT'S STARTING TO FUCKING RAIN!!! DUDE! I CAN'T
BELIEVE IT! WE PANHANDLED ENOUGH FOR A BUTTERFINGER & A
DR. PEPPER. (THE REST IS BUSFARE). FOR BREAKFAST SOMEONE
GAVE US SOME PASTRIES AT BART IN S.F. NOW WE'RE WAITING FOR
THE GILROY BUS. WE HAD TO DITCH THE DR. PEPPER 'CAUSE
HERE'S THE BUS. IT'S NOW 6:35. WE'RE FINALLY IN GILROY! WE'RE
FIENDING FOR A CIGARETTE SO I GUESS WE'LL SMOKE THAN
HIT 101. (THERE'S A S.F. BOUND BUS ACROSS THE STREET, AUGH!)
IT'S 7:15 & WE'RE AT THE ONRAMP. FINALLY. 6 FUCKING HOURS
TO GET HERE. SOMEONE JUST PULLED OVER! OH- OH- OH- HE'S
TOO FAR AWAY - HE'S LEAVING! FUCKING ASSHOLE. WELL, IT'S
8:00. WE QUIT. BESIDES - THERE'S SOME WINGNUT HERE. HE COMES
THEN GOES, COMES THAN GOES. WE SPOKE TO HIM. PRETTY WIERD
GUY. NOW WE'RE AT MCDONALDS PANHANDLING, THEN GOING TO
SLEEP. NO GOOD, NOBODY WANTS TO KICK. DAVE FOUND A DONUT SHOP &
WE ASKED THEM FOR DAY OLD DONUTS & THEY (EVEN BEING
CHINESE!) GAVE US A HALF A DOZEN. I FOUND A SODA CUP
& TOOK IT TO MCDONALDS & TOLD THEM I SPILT MY SODA IN
THE CAR & THEY GAVE ME A NEW COKE! SCAM, SCAM, SCAM.
AFTER THIS - WE'RE GOING TO BED. IT'S ABOUT 8:30. WE'RE
GOING TO THE BATHROOM THEN NIGHTY-NIGHT. OH YEAH, I STARTED
MY PERIOD THIS MORNING. (FRIDAY 9-22-90). LAST NIGHT WHILE
I WAS IN THE BATHROOM, A WINGNUT WANTED TO HITCH WITH
DAVE & FOUND OUT HE WAS WITH ME & WANTED TO GO ANY-
WAY. "WHAT'S A MATTER, DON'T YOU LIKE ME?" DUDE, GO AWAY.
WELL, WE WOKE UP AROUND 2:00 A.M. TO FUCKING RAIN. IT'S
RAINING ON US. SHIT. WE JUST COVERED OUR HEADS & SAID
FUCK IT. WE WOKE UP AT 7. HAD A CIGARETTE (YES, 7 A.M.!) WENT
BACK TO SLEEP, GOT UP AT 7:30 - WENT TO MCDONALDS. I WENT
TO THE BATHROOM & SOME MEXICAN CHICK WORKING THERE
TOOK AN HOUR TO FIX HER HAIR & HAT. SHIT I HAVE TO
BRUSH MY TEETH. I COME OUT, DAVE'S TALKING TO A
LOCAL TRAMP. HE TELLS US NOT TO PANHANDLE -

P62 (9-22-90) THEY'LL KICK YOU OUT OF TOWN & THAT THE TRUCK STOPS OVER THE HILL. HE KEEPS TELLING US TO GO TO CARMEL & SALINAS. THAT'S WHERE ALL THE GOOD DRUGS ARE. HIS NAME WAS DAVE TOO. WE JUST COUNTED 7 FLIES FLYING AROUND THIS TABLE. WE ATE BUTTER FOR BREAKFAST & DAVE THE TRAMP BOUGHT US ALL THE COFFEE WE COULD DRINK. NEXT WE'RE HITTING THE DONUT SHOP. OH YEAH— DAVE THE TRAMP LOST HIS BAG. IT'S 8:45. WE WENT TO THE DONUT SHOP & GOT 7 MORE DONUTS & NOW WE'RE GONNA SMOKE OUR LAST CIGARETTE & GET OUT OF HERE! WELL, IT'S 10:10 & WE'RE GOING TO MCDONALDS TO PEE & GET A CIGARETTE. WE GOT OUR CIGARETTE & WENT TO THE BATHROOM. ME & DAVE ARE CHECKING OUT THIS FINE REDNECK BOY, BLOND & TAN. HEALTHY THING. BYE-BYE HONEY. IT'S 10:35 & WE'RE BACK AT THE RAMP. WELL SITTING HERE, A TRUCK GOES BY & A THING FALLS OFF & ROLLS UP TO US. LOOKS LIKE A HUGE FUCKING ROOT, ABOUT THE SIZE OF MY HEAD. IT HAS A FEW STEMS — LOOKS LIKE IT'S HAIR. I'M GONNA CARVE A FACE ON IT. WE NAMED HIM OGA BOGA & HE TASTES LIKE A GREEN POTATO WITH A LITTLE BIT OF SUGAR. SORRY WE'RE GONNA HAVE TO LEAVE HIM BEHIND. I THINK HE'S DEPRESSED. IT'S 11:11 AND WE FINALLY GOT A RIDE. HER NAME'S DANIELLA, BORN & RAISED IN S.F. LIVES HERE NOW (WHY?) & DRIVES A COOL CAR & LISTENS TO BILLY IDOL. SHE SAYS SHE'S ONLY GOING TO SAN JUAN. WHEREVER THAT IS. OH SHIT. SHE DROPS US OFF ON THE WATSONVILLE EXIT (I THINK IT'S 126 OR 129) THIS IS HELL. I'VE BEEN HERE BEFORE. NO CARS COME THRU. ON THE BACK OF THE SIGN IT SAYS "YOU WILL BE HERE AT LEAST 5 HOURS— ENJOY!" IT'S 11:24. WE FOUND SOME CORN. OH MY GOD. A VAN PULLING OVER. THEY MUST NEED DIRECTIONS. WE GOT A RIDE, HOLY SHIT. IT'S 11:30. IT'S 11:35 WE'RE AT THE SAN JUAN BAUTISTA EXIT. IT WAS SOME ARTIST DUDE & HIS CONNECTICUT HIPPIE GIRLFRIEND. WHEN WE GET OUT OF THE VAN HE GOES "GOOD SPEED." I'M LIKE, WHAT? "OH, I MEAN GOD SPEED." I WONDER WHAT'S ON HIS MIND. I DON'T KNOW IF THIS IS BETTER OR WORSE. IT SURE IS WINDY. SO FAR EVERYONE'S A FUCKING NON— SMOKER & WE HAVE NO CIGARETTES. IT'S 12:00 & SOMEONE JUST FLIPPED US OFF. IT'S 12:22. WE GOT A RIDE. HE'S GOING TO SALINAS, DOESN'T SMOKE. 12:40, WE'RE IN SALINAS. 330 MILES FROM L.A. WELL, IT'S ALL MEXICANS HERE, DUDE. WE FOUND A MOTEL HELL (LA MOTEL DE HELL) & GOT THE FUCK OUT. WE BOUGHT OUR SMOKES & 2 LICORICES. NOW WE'RE PANHANDLING. A SEVERE WHITE BOY DEATH ~~——~~ WISH HERE. "NO NADA." TWO HARLEYS DROVE BY AND I RAISED MY THUMB— YEAH! DUMB THING TO DO HERE SURROUNDED BY IMMIGRANTS. WELL, WE MADE $8 SO FAR. WELL, WE MADE $33 — GOT 6 MORE LICORICES. THEN SPLIT. HERE WE ARE AT THE ONRAMP. IT'S 1:36. IT'S 2:10 & DAVE, TRYING TO DO AN OGA BOGA CHANT TO GET US OUT OF HERE (HE'S NOW OUR HITCHHIKING GOD) DISCOVERED THE SACRED COP CHANT. HE STOPPED CHANTING. WELL NOW IT'S 3:46 AND SOME W.A.S.P. BABY BITCH JUST STUCK HER

(9-22-90) TONGUE OUT AT US. EARLIER SOME NIGGERS DROVE BY & SAID "YOU WANT A RIDE, IT'LL COST YOU MONEY." PEOPLE HAVE BEEN DRIVING BY WAIVING, SMILING OR POINTING AT THEIR DASHBOARD OR POINTING AHEAD WILDLY. ME & DAVE DECIDED IF WE GET STUCK HERE WE'RE NOT GOING INTO TOWN TO EAT. NO WAY WE'RE GONNA CLIMB TREES, ACT LIKE LEAVES, CATCH BYRDS & EAT THEM. ITS 4:00 & WE JUST GOT PICKED UP BY A MEXICAN IN A FUCKED UP 260Z. WE JUST PULLED OVER FOR A SECOND SO HE CAN FIX IT. THE POINTS ARE FUCKED UP. DAVE'S GOT THE BACK AREA. NO SEAT. HE'S SCRUNCHED. THE CAR KEEPS STALLING ON THE FREEWAY. THE GUY OFFERS ME 10$ FOR A BLOW JOB & DAVE CAN PRETEND HE'S ASLEEP! OH SHIT. WE DON'T TRUST THIS GUY AT ALL. HE'S TAKING THE BACK WAY & BREAKING DOWN. PHEW. WE'RE FINALLY THERE. GONZALEZ. ITS 4:34. THERE'S A WHOLE 3,000 PEOPLE HERE. WE SAW LIGHTNIN' WE HEARD THUNDER. OH SHIT, ITS RAINING. THAT'S BEFORE WE GOT OUT OF THAT GUYS CAR. NOW WE'RE HERE AT BURGER QUEEN PANHANDLING (THEY SELL TACOS & BURRITOS). THERE'S COWBOYS & MEXICANS HERE. I THINK THE GAS STATIONS GONNA FALL APART. TWO MEXICANS CAME BY & ONE GAVE US A DOLLAR & ON THEIR WAY OUT THE OTHER ONE GAVE US ANOTHER DOLLAR SO WE GOT A BURRITO & A SODA. NOW WE HAVE 22¢. ITS STILL THUNDERING & LIGHTNING, BUT NO RAIN YET. I HOPE WE CAN GET OUT OF HERE. WE WENT TO THE ONRAMP. THE SKY WAS PRETTY DARK. WE TALKED TO SOME BILLY GOATS AT THE SIDE THEN IT STARTED RAINING. WE CHECKED UNDER THE BRIDGE & IT LOOKS PRETTY COOL SO BACK OVER TO BURGER QUEEN. WE ASKED A GUY IF HE COULD SPARE SOME CHANGE FOR COFFEE. HE SAID HE'D THINK ABOUT IT. HE CAME OUT & HANDED US $2.00 SO WE WENT INSIDE & HAD COFFEE & A HAMBURGER. THEY'RE OUT OF BURRITOS. OH YEAH- WE WASTED 2 CIGARETTES ON THAT MEXICAN "I WANT A 10 DOLLAR BLOW JOB" DUDE. OH YEAH. WHEN WE WERE SITTING THERE BEFORE THAT DUDE GAVE US 2.00 - A BIG ASS LIGHTNING FLASHED BEFORE US. A SECOND LATER THE THUNDER CLAPPED SO FUCKING LOUD I FELT LIKE I WAS HAVING A HEART ATTACK FROM THE VIBRATIONS, IT WAS PRETTY LONG TOO. I PICKED MY NOSE & WIPED THE BIGGEST BOGER EVER UNDER THIS TABLE WE SIT AT. BACK TO PALO ALTO STANFORD SHOPPING CENTER, 3 LADIES WALKED BY AND THE YOUNGEST ONE SAYS "I USED MY NEW HAND CREAM LAST NIGHT." THEN THE MIDDLE OLD LADY SAYS "THANK-YOU FOR THAT INPUT." AND THEY THINK WE HAVE WIERD WAYS OF TALKING. ITS 6:10 NOW & WE'RE GONNA TRY HITCHHIKING AGAIN. IT STARTED RAINING AGAIN BUT STOPPED. I SAW LIGHTNING HIT THE MOUNTAIN & STARTED A FIRE BUT IT WENT OUT. ITS 7:30 & DARK SO NOW WE'RE PANHANDLING FOR A PACK OF SMOKES. THERE'S STILL LIGHTNING BUT NO THUNDER OR RAIN. I JUST SAW A HUGE FUCKING FLY BUT IT WAS A GRASS-HOPPER. SHIT. ITS ONLY 8:00 & THE GAS STATIONS CLOSING. I CAN'T BELIEVE IT. WELL, I GUESS WE GO TO BED. GOOD NIGHT. WE'RE WALKING HOME & FOUND A TIN CAN COOKER IN THE PARKING LOT ENTRANCE.

PG. 4 (9-22-90) WE DECIDED TO GO TO BURGER QUEEN & WROTE "WASH ME"
ON THE SIGN. IT WAS PRETTY DIRTY. WE'RE TRYING TO GET A CIGARETTE
NOW WE'RE GOING HOME. WE BUMMED A PEN (BUNK) FROM BURGER QUEEN
BEFORE WE LEFT. SUNDAY, SEPT. 23 1990. IT'S 9:00 AM AND WE'RE UP.
WE'RE AT THE GAS STATION AND WE USED A TOILET TOKEN FROM
C.J.S FOR THE BATHROOM. A DUDE DROVE UP IN A HELICOPTER &
WOULDN'T GIVE DAVE A CIGARETTE OR CHANGE. ANOTHER MEXICAN
US 2 CIGARETTES. ANOTHER MEXICAN HAD NO MONEY. ANOTHER
MEXICAN GAVE US A DOLLAR & ONE GAVE US A QUARTER.
OH YEAH, IT WAS STILL RAINING WHEN WE GOT UP. WE GOT
2 MORE CIGARETTES FROM ANOTHER MEXICAN & I ASKED
FOR SOME CHANGE & THE OTHER ASKED HOW MUCH SO I
ASKED FOR $75 & HE GAVE ME ALL HIS CHANGE THEN IN
THE STORE HE WALKED UP TO US & GAVE US ANOTHER $3.00
THEN WHEN WE WERE PAYING FOR OUR STUFF HE GAVE US
ANOTHER $2.00. HE WAS CUTE TOO. SO WE BOUGHT 2 BIG BURRITOS,
A PACK OF CIGARETTES & A SODA & STILL HAVE $2.00
LEFT. WE THANK THE OGA BOGA GOD OF HITCHIKING WE
LEFT IN GILROY FACING TRAFFIC. WE WERE GONNA GET A
SODA & CANDY BAR AT 11:30 BUT WE GOT A RIDE AT 11:28.
THE GUYS GOING TO FUCKING L.A.! PRAISE OGA BOGA! WE
LISTENED TO PINK FLOYD THEN CHEAP RAP, STOPPED IN SAN
LUIS OBISPO FOR GAS & A SODA & A CANDY BAR. THE DUDES
DOIN' 85-90 MPH. WE STOPPED IN SANTA BARBARA TO
DROP OFF HIS SHIT & HE PLAYS FUCKING HINDU MUSIC!
WELL, HERE WE ARE, SUNSET BY UCLA. WE'RE GONNA
CHECK OUT HOLIDAY INNS BATHROOM. OH YEAH, ANOTHER
NON-SMOKER. IT'S 4:00. IT'S 4:28. DAVE GOT KICKED OUT
OF HOLIDAY INN & NOW WE'RE WAITING FOR THE #2
BUS TO TAKE US HOME. WELL IT'S 5:30 & WE'RE
FINALLY HOME— HOLLYWOOD.
                              THE END.

Party Hardy,
Rock & Roll
Drink a fifth
Smoke a bowl
I got some problems I can settle
All I need is....
Heavy Metal
Nikki
Pinky!!!!
Here I sit my buns a flexin giving birth to another Texan!
Good Night!
Nikki
Pinky
Russ
D.W.
Rick
Tweeky Dave
Ziggy
&
John Boy
Nikki
-Loves-
Russ B.

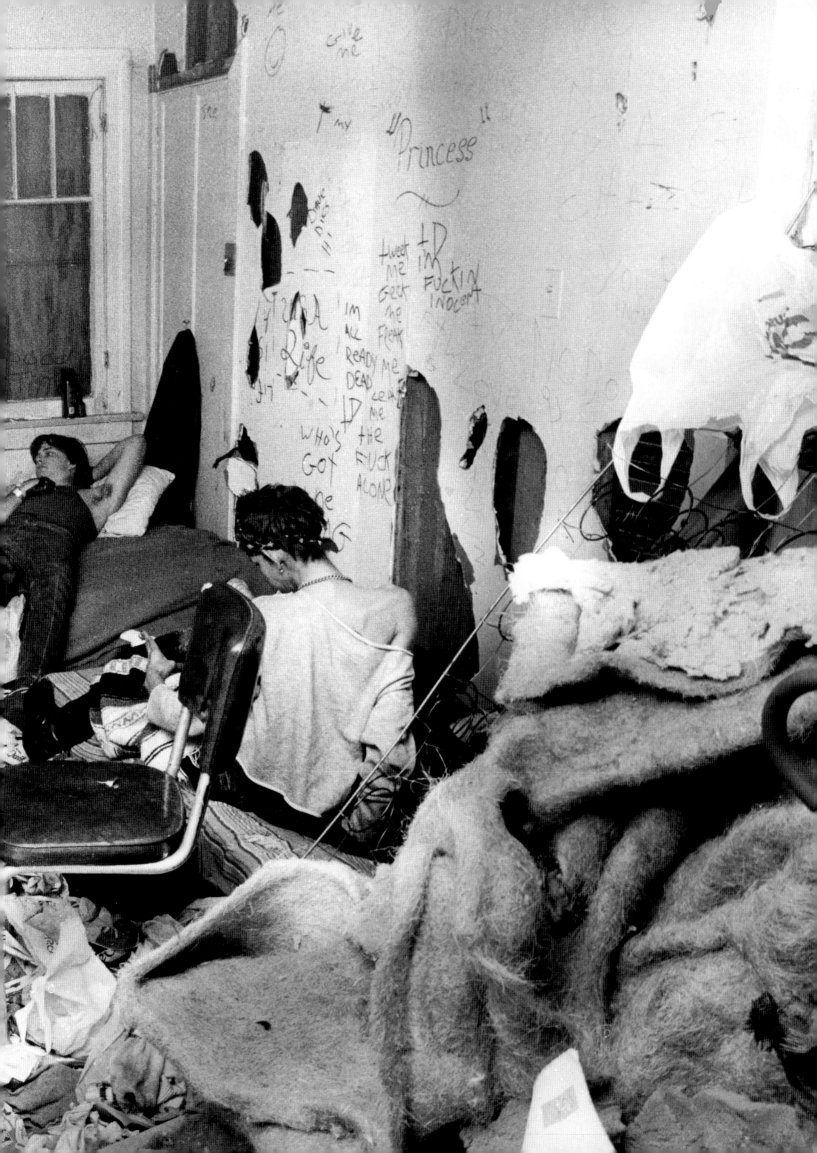

January 21, San Francisco

Echo's mom calls. She asks if I've heard from her.

January 27

The phone rings. Echo and Dave are in Hollywood. Echo wants me to drive down there now. Tears.

> **Echo:** We're both sick, slamming heroin, sleepin' on bus benches. Now I have a drug record.
>
> **Dave:** I'm worried about her, man. She scratches and shakes a lot. I am dying. Someone's gotta help us. Now!

April 15, Marcos goes to New York

There's a message on the machine.

> **Marcos:** Hi, it's me and I want out. Brad and I are leaving today for New York. Call you from there. Bye.

Marcos ends up in Salt Lake City two days later, crying on the phone, scared, because he is the only black kid prostitute in Utah and no one will touch him. Brad is getting dates but he's slamming all the profits. Marcos says he needs $50 for a ticket to Chicago. Says he wants to see Oprah and tell her his problems. Says he has a $3,000 a week job, strip dancing, waiting for him in DC and some man promised him a date with a real senator.

> **Marcos:** I'll do anything for you if you can just help me this one last time.

I send him the money.

April 19

Marcos calls. He's drunk and says he's been that way since he got to Chicago.

April 22

There's another message from Marcos. He's in jail. There's a phone number to call. I am connected to an officer, who tells me they arrested a minor, Mr. Lynch, in order to protect him.

> **Officer:** He was so drunk he threw up on a john while threatening him with a knife. It's not safe for him to be on the streets of Chicago.
>
> **Marcos:** It's all my fault, Jim, 'cause I lost Brad's stuff, his clothes and everything. He has a serious drug problem and he's slamming all our money. I think Brad left for New York without me. When I get out of jail, I'm going to follow him. And if I can't find Brad, at least I'll get famous. I'm good and I'll prove it.

April 29

We get a collect call from Marcos. Like the stereotypical tourist monologue, he goes on and on about sightseeing in New York City.

> **Marcos:** Hi, Jim. Here I am in the Big Apple. Honey, it's soooo big, you wouldn't believe it. I've seen everything — Greenwich Village, the Statue of Liberty, Madison Square Garden, the Empire State Building, and Grand Central — from the outside, mind you. I'm staying at the Greyhound station. Haven't slept yet. I'm gonna go down to Christopher Street and hustle for a week. Then I'll get a job at Burger King. I wish I could find Brad.

April 30

Marcos calls again. He met a guy named Jerry or Joe, he's not sure which. He met him at the Trump Tower. He's an architectural historian. Marcos might go home with him.

May Day

Marcos's bag — with his coat, sweater, books, tapes, toothbrush, everything — was stolen by a date who beat him up. Marcos wants to come home to go to school. He's looking in the mirror and says he looks dead. He asks me to pray for him. Marcos wants more money and he's pissed when I tell him that it seems he only calls when he needs something (money). I told him how to get to a shelter so that he would have a place to sleep.

Next day

> **Marcos:** I found a job delivering flowers. I'm sleeping at the shelter, but it's so crowded that I have to sit up to go to sleep. I'm lonely, Jim. Been goin' to church. It helps. I heard Brad was around. I'm checking out all the whore corners.

May 8

> **Marcos:** I found Brad in jail for pimpin' and panderin'. He has a $300,000 bail 'cause the DA wants him to talk about some "very important people that he has been associating with." The DA knows Brad has a lot to say.

Marcos wants me to go to Polk Street to find Terry, the queen, who is supposed to have the number of a sugardaddy with lots of money. Maybe he can bail Brad out of jail.

> **Marcos:** If Brad talks they will kill him. And maybe me too. After Brad gets out, we're going to have a big party and everyone's invited and everyone can take a big hit off a big rock. And we all will be high, high, high. Then I'll love Brad 'til he's dead.

May 25

Marcos calls. He's in Hollywood with Brad.

>**Marcos:** I don't believe we made it back alive. God, I love New York. Brad sold a bracelet he got from a date for $1,300. We bought the bus tickets for $300 and smoked the rest. When we were about half way across the country, we got so lost we couldn't find ourselves or our luggage. But now everything is so sweet, girl. I'm hustling so I can save a lot money to go to school, get my teeth fixed, and get glasses.

June 5

>**Marcos:** Brad stole the rent money to get high. No one has seen him since. I'm homeless. I think he's dead. Too bad, 'cause I loved him. You know I did.

June 16

Marcos calls. Brad's alive and well. Marcos found him, sick from speed, puking and having hallucinations in a park. It was Brad's third gram in a week. Marcos was also coming down from a seven day binge. He was sitting on a bench and Brad told Marcos he loved him. Marcos fell off the bench into dog shit. Then Brad said he'd come right back, but now it's been three hours. Their stuff is sitting in some hotel and they have 'til eleven o'clock to get it out. All they need is $50. And on and on and on....

San Francisco

The doorbell's buzzing, won't let up. It's raining hard. We know it must be Tank. Blade and Psycho are with him. All three are wrapped in one wet blanket. They have a dog. It smells. They hug it, then hit it. They smell too. Tank has been badly beaten. His face is ugly and all cut up. One eye is black with a purple sunset all around. They are like scared little children who just want to come in off the street. I give them a ride to the Civic Center camps — safer territory. They get out of the car but the stench won't go away. These kids are becoming bums.

Civic Center camps

Facing City Hall is a long rectangular reflecting pool that divides a set of olive trees and park benches. Interspersed between them are separate huddles of the homeless: the old-timers, the blacks, the Indians, the immigrants, the queens, the hippie/punks, and the Dogs. Within a fifteen foot area I am surrounded by four or five ghetto blasters, each blowing its own different discord. A tall boy is playing an unplugged electric guitar while a crazed girl argues with herself about something, anything. It's growing cold. Cigarettes make our only light as everyone settles into the darkness. Lorna is in the reflecting pool, meekly trying to drown herself because Tank has broken up with her.

> **Tank:** It's because I'm following the rainbow and I don't want to be tied down to one girl.

Tank is high on speed and says that he is the new leader of the Dogs and that everyone should call him Thorn. Most people are too fucked-up to argue. Thorn says that Tank died when he climbed up a skyscraper and jumped off the top into a cup of blood. He points to a building in the distance. His arm is covered with fresh cigarette burns.

Doug and Blade, Room 412, The Bristol Hotel

The street outside is full of plastic rings pretending to be gold. Blade and Doug are hiding out from a bad dope deal, owing money on bunk shit. Cornered in this small room, both are jonesin'— crashin' hard. Blade has aged. Her face and flesh hang too thin off her body. She is wearing a polyester halter top, attempting glamour but coming up street, like someone who walks through hotel halls, trying to remember which room she is sleeping in tonight. She is stretched across a mutilated bed. Depressed? Bored? Doug is tall, maybe 34 and funny looking, with a big Harley-Davidson tattoo across his back. He talks incessantly, nasalizing like Daffy Duck, about how big and bad he is. Simultaneously, he reminds me that he knows that he sounds like the coyote character who is always getting blown up in the cartoons. Doug is talking to himself by the sink in the corner.

> **Blade:** He hits me. I don't know how to get out of it. This is the best I can do for now, Jim. I miss Tank.

Im Falling No gravity In my Life

Li ke Dust SWEPt Under the CARPet

Monday

Dave and Echo have hitched up to San Francisco, saying they're tired of their Hollywood existence and need a change. They are squatting at Civic Center, next camp over from the Dogs. They are excited to see me and tell me that I am like a good drug (all roads lead to the same place). They are with Tiny Waller, a geeky, red-headed kid with a mohawk, who drawls a brag about how much drinking and drugs he's done today with Thorn. Echo says she's been happy for the past twenty-four hours, ever since she started going out with Tiny Waller. Tiny says that the happiest he's ever been was when he got outta jail and he and Cookie went through a quarter ounce in two days. Dave pretends that he doesn't care, but brazenly confides that he wishes Tiny were dead and Echo was in his arms. Echo thinks of Dave as a flea hopping around her face, annoying her to no end.

Tuesday

A mohawk punk gives all three of them tattoos. Tiny puts "Echo" and "FTW" (Fuck the World) on his chest. Echo has "Tiny" written on the back of her neck. Dave gets "Echo," an anarchy sign, and "FTW" (Fuck Tiny Waller) written on his arms.

Wednesday night

The door buzzes and Echo arrives, unexpectedly. She needs our bathroom. She has twigs and leaves stuck in her hair and says that she's been lost, tweeking in hell. She leaves abruptly. Later, just as suddenly, Echo returns, bleeding from her neck where she tried to scratch off the "Tiny" tattoo. I give her some first aid ointment and a place to rest.

> **Echo:** Tiny told me that he would love me forever and then the asshole walks away with another girl.

Then Dave calls in despair, howling that he's tied to Echo like an umbilical cord that can't be broken.

> **Dave:** Where's Echo? I fuckin' swear I'm gonna have to pound Tiny Waller's face.

Friday

Dave is on four hits of acid. He is not wearing a shirt and appears even thinner than I remember, his scar popping out. I share a cigarette with him, then notice blisters on his mouth. Echo's hair is matted. She is wearing glasses that aren't hers with lenses that keep falling out. She tries to sleep in the corner, fetal-positioned on our couch, saying repeatedly, "no one understands," and "I give up." Challenging Dave to combat, she argues with him about who will die sooner. He just wants to talk classical music.

> **Dave:** Dude, Mozart is sooooo....

Monday

I take Echo and Dave to the hospital pediatric clinic. Both are on speed and they hate being inside the doctor's office.

> **Intake worker:** Date of birth?
>
> **Dave:** February 26, '72.
>
> **Intake worker:** Where are you staying?
>
> **Dave:** Nowhere. The streets.
>
> **Intake worker:** Social security number?
>
> **Dave:** 466-25-4033.
>
> **Intake worker:** Do you have any family?
>
> **Dave:** No. I got a really bad cold, though.

A doctor enters and begins to examine Dave.

> **Doc:** Blood?
>
> **Dave:** Yeah. Just streaks.
>
> **Doc:** Any fever?
>
> **Dave:** Yesterday. I live on the streets so it's kinda hard to tell. I felt really bad yesterday but the drugs help. I use a lot of drugs.
>
> **Doc:** IV?
>
> **Dave:** Yeah.
>
> **Doc:** How do you protect yourself from AIDS?
>
> **Dave:** I don't really. If I have the bleach, I'll use it. If I have a new rig, I'll use it. But if I wanna get high and there's a rig there, I'll use it.
>
> **Doc:** Do you eat?
>
> **Dave:** Between getting high and not feeling good, I eat pretty sporadically.
>
> **Doc:** You have some congestion in your chest. We should watch it. Do you smoke a lot?
>
> **Echo:** Whenever he can.
>
> **Doc:** I want to put you on erythromycin. Anything else?
>
> **Dave:** Not unless you're giving away free dope.
>
> **Echo:** Yeah, I'll take something for my psoriasis and some amphetamines.

By the next day their medicine is lost and their moods turn more sour. I take them to the highway goin' south. Dave says Echo let him sleep next to her last night and maybe that means she'll have him.

> **Dave:** What do you think is gonna happen to us?

Christmas day

It's cold. A homicidal wind is blowing. We are all huddled up under tarps as some drunk, cross-eyed guy shows us proof that he was a Supreme Court Justice and offers Blade $100 to fuck him. Thorn chases him away. The rains come and everyone scrambles to

find shelter in the loading docks. Thorn is just out of jail, depressed because Blade
finally broke up with him. Sick from tweek and beer, he is puking into a paper bag while
swearing that he is going to get a job.

Blade: Fuck it. The only time he ever talks about getting a job is when we break up.
I don't care about him anymore because slamming speed is a hell of a lot better.

I have to piss and Blade points to the spot right next to her. In the corner is a branch
acting as a Christmas tree with a broken doll filling in for the angel and a beer
can perched on top in place of the guiding star. Arley is talking and won't stop. Nobody
listens. Dopey is scavenging through some other dude's bag. Bear wants to start a fight
with his stump of an arm. Sativa is drunk, trying to open cans of food with a knife,
sucking out cold beans and applesauce. Molly from LA is looking for dope. Weedhopper
is trying to find an inner tube for a bike he just stole. Mark comes by, just looking
for someone to talk to. Finally, José arrives and sits next to Wolfette. He nudges her
until there are smiles and giggles between them and something simply happens.
A merry Christmas for some.

Hustling, Sunset Boulevard, Hollywood

Kid #1: I get in the car with him and we're drivin' around. And I act all innocent, askin' like, "Why did you pick me up?" And he says, "I'm just lonely." And I'm looking at his car and thinking dollar signs. I say, "Let's get to the price range." I tell him a sob story about how my last trick ripped me off so I gotta have half of it up front. He gives it to me and I reassure him, all nice and shit, talkin' 'bout how I'm so young and innocent. And I say, "Don't worry, I'm gonna do you good." Then when he hits the first stop sign I'm like, zzzump, out of the car. He grabs my shirt and says, "Gimme my money back." I hit him in the mouth and take off. I know it's not right.

Kid #2: Last night I was watching TV and it's this show about politics. I see this guy on it and I realize I know him. I spent a weekend with the dude, sittin' in his house smokin' hubbas and drinkin' beer — me and four other girls. See, he had forty rocks and $500 hidden for each of us. At least that's what he said. And he said, "Go find them and then make daddy happy." And I was already tripping and shit. So when I looked at his dick it was all wrinkled and shit. And I, like, didn't care 'cause all I could think about was the rock and the money. I sucked him off real good a bunch of times. Stayed so high it ain't funny.

Kid #3: Yesterday we were panhandling and my girlfriend asked this guy in a suit for spare change and he goes, "Well, you can come home with me and I'll give you a place to sleep and a hot meal. All you have to do is my dishes." So we said, "Okay." And we're in the car with him and he goes to us, "Do you like to get high?" And we're like going, "Why not?" And we do. Then he asks me if I want to make twenty extra bucks keeping bowling scores. So I went and kept score for this league for like five hours. While I was gone he had her at his house and kept asking her all these damn questions like, would she ever fuck around on me? The guy was doing cocaine and he gave her some. When I got back he told me, "If you want to stay here, you're going to have to get a job and give me half your paycheck." And I was like, "Fuck you. I left home 'cause they were fucking telling me what to do." This morning we were goin' through his photo album and we saw all these pictures of naked girls. I knew his deal. He was going to get us all coked-up and take pictures of her. So we left a note that said, "Thanks but no thanks." We could've taken his shit — TV, VCRs — but didn't.

Kid #4: This john stops and asks, "Do you pull dates?" And I says, "Maybe." And we start talkin' and he asks, "So what do you do?" And I say, "Well, mostly everything." Then I jump in and we drive around and talk and I give him a hand job. And then he gives me $100. It's easy to live like that. But it never lasts. Next time I go with him he starts beating up on me while I'm fucking him. Crystal jumped out of a hotel window trying to get away from the same guy. She broke both her legs.

wearin yesterdays misfortune Like A crown

Next year, October 26, San Francisco

Echo's mom calls. She is worried.

R. Sylvia: It's my birthday and Beth hasn't phoned. It's unlike her.

The last R. Sylvia heard, Echo was in room 325 at the West Hotel. R. Sylvia wants me to try to find her. The lobby of the West Hotel is empty except for a couple nodding out in a corner and two young wanna-be dope dealers trying to call a connect, collect, to get drugs on credit. Someone started a fire in the elevator and the manager is attempting to put it out. Two seven-year-olds are running up and down the stairs, playing tag. I knock on the door of room 325. A sign says, "No visitors without Frank's permission." Knock again.

Man: What do you want?

Jim: Echo.

Man: She ain't here.

Jim: Well, tell Frank to tell Echo that Jim stopped by.

I return later. There is a new sign announcing, "The circus is over, no more performers need apply. STAY AWAY unless you have business." The door is cracked open. I enter and see Echo with this very young, prematurely ancient whore, sitting in this thrashed out room trying to put on fake nails. Their teeth are grinding as they file the plastic nails on a stone. They stick their fingers in glue, their hands contorting, to put on the nails. Then they rip them off and place them on backwards. Confusing the order, they give up and try to sniff the glue.

Whore: Well, I'm pretty fucked-up.

Echo: Nah. I've tweeked harder.

The TV is blaring. A man (Frank) walks in and out of the room, going in circles and talking dope deal gibberish.

Frank: This is bunk dope. Let's call it "Wah Wah Bad."

All three of them begin talking the "Wah Wah Bad" dope talk. They think it's cool, although I can't follow their conversation. Echo states that she wants to quit dope "cause she's in love, except that she can't since she's so stressed because her new boyfriend Doug is in jail and they have a $400 phone bill. She shows me a picture of them together. The Polaroid has writing on the white borders: "Echo & Doug" and "I Love You Baby." In the photo, Doug is sitting behind Echo, his arms around her mistrustingly. He is the same coyote cartoon-faced Doug who I met with Blade. Frank starts throwing the phone around the room. Increasingly upset, he needs to call his connect real bad. Sales shit.

Frank: This fucking phone is bunk.

Whore: I think that phone must be evil. The devil's on the line.

Frank and Echo agree. I take the telephone and switch it on. I become like a magician to them. Frank quickly calls in for his drug messages. The whore shows off her nails, some on backwards and very crooked, glued tight. Echo gives up on the fake ones and is now biting her own nails down to a stubble.

A week later, Doug calls me from San Bruno County Jail.

> **Doug:** Hello Jim. Echo gave me your number. I haven't heard from her in five days. If she don't get my shit to Christina this week I'm going to break every fuckin' bone in her body when I get out. And tell her I got VD from her.

Later

I meet Echo in the Economy Restaurant. She is sketching hard, her sentences incomplete. Like a knife whose edge has been lost, she is listless and dull. Echo is wearing red sunglasses glued and taped together, so scratched that she can't see out of them. Blood is leaking from her psoriasis-scarred arms. I buy her breakfast but Echo is nodding from dope and can't eat. She's been slamming all the dope she got bag chasing, earned from dates with people whose names she can't even remember. She's been forgetting whether or not she's cleaned the points. One guy she's been with even has AIDS and she doesn't care. She certainly can't be bothered waiting for Doug, a "stupid, motherfucking, girl-crazed asshole," to get out of jail.

> **Echo:** There are other dudes with bags of dope who are onto me. I need to survive, to be protected.

Echo laughs — a twangy, insipid cackle — then cries. She wishes she could see her mom but can't handle the pressure. She impresses on me that she would like to take care of herself, but is almost at the point of no return.

One week later

Now out of jail, Doug is already gaunt and he's broken parole. He's with Echo and they've been dealing bunk dope and jonesin' out of a hotel room obtained with a stolen credit card. She says they are not getting along anymore. Doug is visibly hurt by her comment and quacks back in his cartoon voice:

> **Doug:** Girl, why you done tell him that? You know I've been stressin' over us. We need money for food and clothes.
>
> **Echo:** I don't want anything but the dope.

It's raining and she gives me that "sick of it all" look. I can't offer them much since her only mission now is to get high in order to get through another day. I can't stand the fact that I am chronicling Echo's destruction and I can't do anything to help.

The next day, Doug gets busted again, this time for resisting arrest, sale, and carrying a dangerous weapon. The DA says that he'll be sent to San Quentin. Weary of the street and all these forlorn hopes — with never-ending nothing-but-downhill-from-here stories — I am very sad and want to escape to my own comfortable world. I run into Tweeky Dave on the street.

> **Dave:** Echo's been showing her tits to everyone but me. Fuck it. If that girl ain't careful she'll be dead by Christmas and I haven't even gotten to fuck her yet.

Dave wants to talk Echo into going home to her mom's house.

> **Dave:** I'd follow her home, Jim. How can I tell her I love her? Maybe you can help me.

Tank

Tank calls saying he's back from somewhere, drunk on Night Train, and tripping hellaciously on twenty four hits of acid. He says he ain't Tank or Thorn no more. Now he's Sean, the name he was born with, and Sean wants to find Blade and go straight (like me), grow his hair long, move to Milwaukee, go to wrestling school, and start a rock and roll band. He needs money and a lawyer because he's in jail again. He is panicked and promises me anything if I will help to get him released.

There's a message from Doug on the machine. He put his arm through a window in San Quentin and cut up some nerves. He wants me to tell Echo something, anything nice, that would convince her to like him again.

Carl's Jr., San Francisco

Jim: I heard from your old boyfriend.

Echo: Which one, Dave? Word's out that he OD'd on some beach in Mexico from all his TV talk show profits. Motherfucker still owes me for a bike he stole. I think he's still jealous of Ziggy or Doug.

Jim: Doug is my guess. He's the one who called.

Echo: I don't know that person anymore. He's really wigged-out. He calls me three times a day from jail — $2,000 in phone bills. I told him, "Look, I can't deal with you anymore." What does he want from me anyway? He got two letters from me and that's the most anybody has gotten in five years. Hell, I still haven't written my mom.

Jim: You know your mom called me?

Echo: Really? How come every time I hear "Love is a Battlefield" I want to go home? Doo baby doo. My mom's cool, actually. Me and her get along a lot better now. She's a lot like me. Gets blinded by shit.

Jim: She doesn't always know what to do with you.

Echo: I don't always know what to do with her, either. Then again, I don't always know what to do with me. Why should she? I'm gonna go back and see her, but first I'm going down to LA. I gotta see if Dave's still alive and if Ziggy's out of prison yet.

Jim: You turning tricks?

Echo: No.

Jim: Dancing?

Echo: No. Not enough money. They wanted me to do a lesbian love act.

Jim: So how are you surviving?

Echo: A run here, a run there. I have a couple good connections. Might go on GA.

Jim: What do you think is going to happen to you?

Echo: I don't know. I suppose I'll live — eventually I'll die.

Jim: When is your doctor's appointment?

Echo: Next week.

Jim: Promise me you'll let me know the results?

Echo: Promise. I got to run, Jim.

Civic Center camps

Lorna is sitting on a garbage can in front of the library, hustling while holding a "peace" flower. Loaded and Germ are looking for a "hell of a lot of drugs," while Red Man is so geeked he can't speak. Freckie is lying across a bench playing the guitar. He gets up to shake my hand and fill me in on what's up.

Freckie: Kristy is in New Orleans doing porno films and thinks she'll be the next Marilyn Monroe 'cause she has great tits. Jersey Lu's in Oklahoma. She had Cruise's baby. Green Racho is a bike messenger and Purple Racho is squatting in Sacramento. Adam and Troy have AIDS. Scooter is dead. Kelly gave up her kid and is hanging out in bars on Polk Street selling pot. Mad Max is still trying to hustle but no one will fuck him 'cause he's all bones and too spun from speed. Deion hasn't been seen for months. The word is he's in some witness protection program while helping prosecute some former hotel hot shot who likes little boys and girls. Doc's in San Quentin for the rest of his life. Animal got five years, no parole, and is sick from the "warm apple sauce jail food."

Wez runs over, interrupting. He heard that Calvin was found dead in his hotel room. He starts talking shit about how he's now a skin who "works undercover." Wez wants to reminisce about "the good ol' racist days." He heads down the street smoking a joint, hoping to scrounge up enough change for some breakfast. Anne-Marie waves me over to say that there is magic everywhere, pointing to some small cherry tomatoes growing under the sewer grate, her "secret garden in hell." She tells me that she saw Dave on a TV talk show.

Anne-Marie: Dave's alive and lookin' so good now that he's famous. I dreamed about fucking him.

Sleezy old men

Jack'n off in front of me
you have to get high to do it

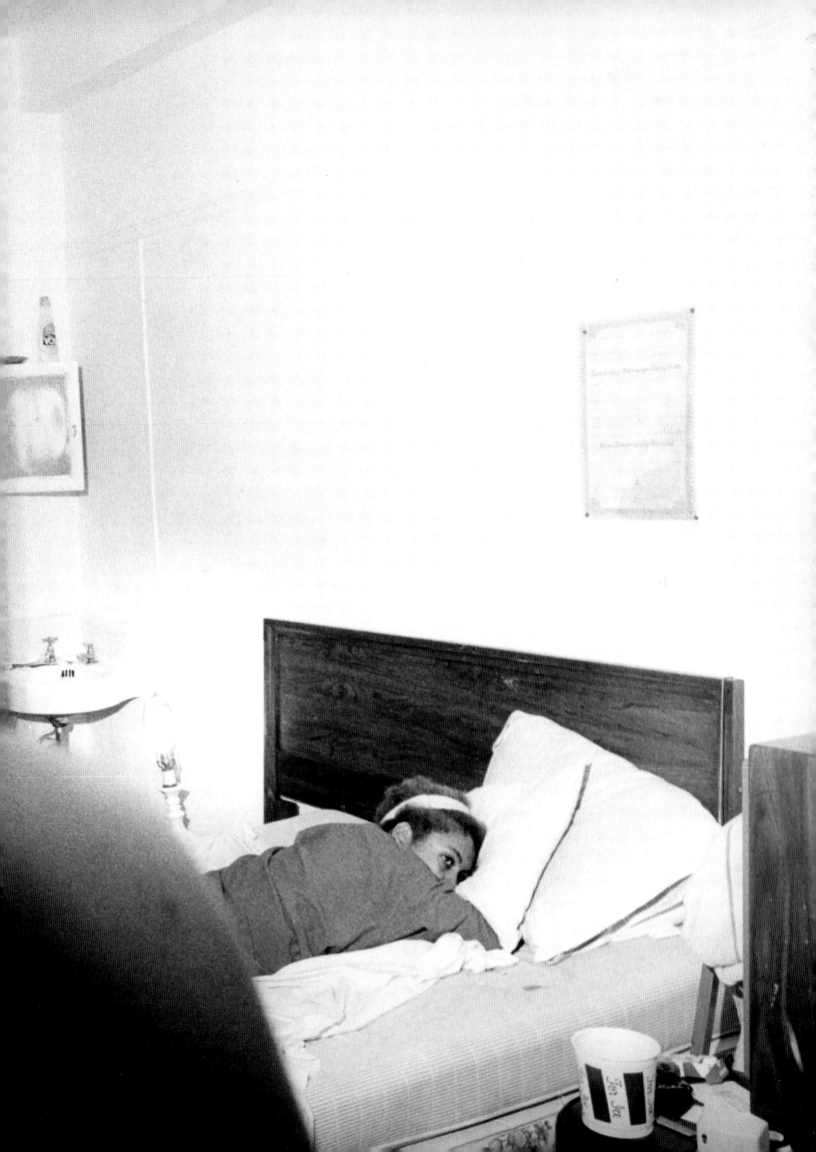

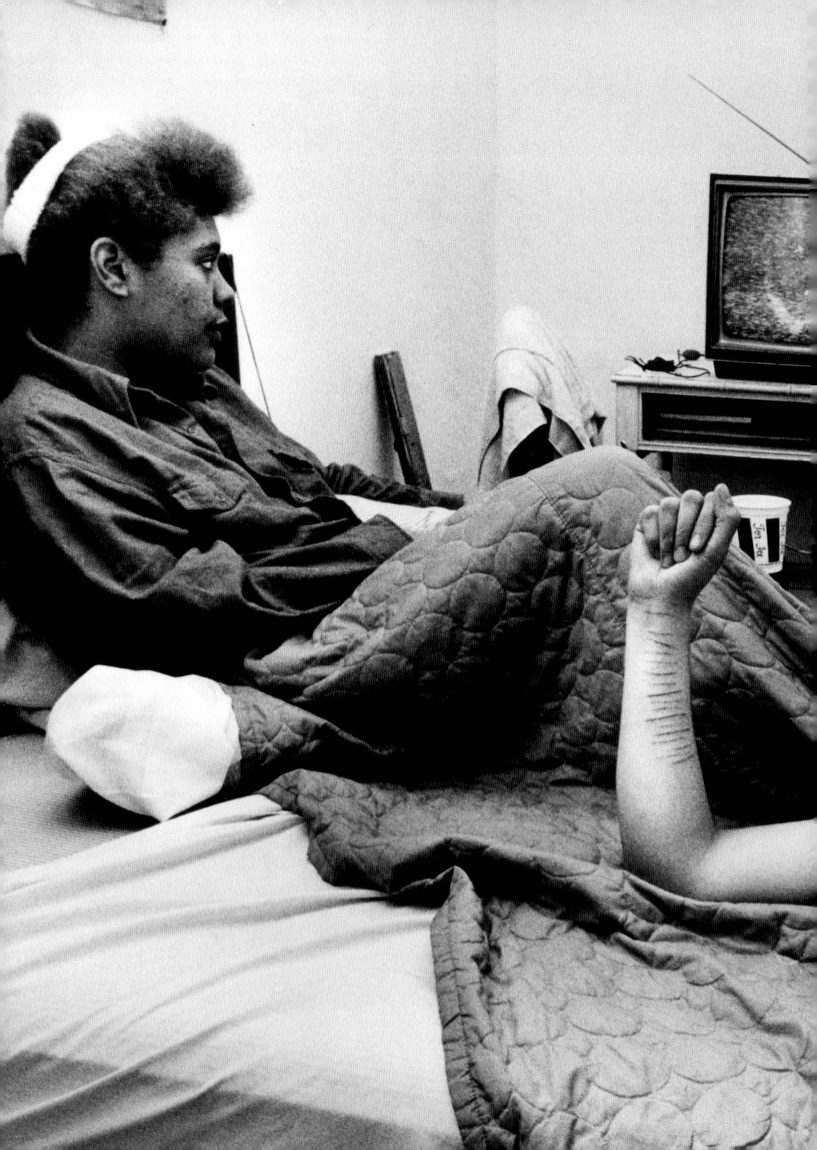

She was passed out drunk and he kept offering me drinks. I refused he woke her up. they played with

kissing each other for the camera. A tone was being set something to happen. Shewanted tochange

into her bathing suit, his shirt to come off. . I had been warned from his phone call. And what

Cornell had said. . More drinking. Trips to the bathroom , clothes off. Not knowing what to do

They didnt believe me whne I said I didnt want fucking pictures. I figured I could try to take

of fucking!

pictures without their faces. He was becoming hesitant! She taunted him. more drinking. a charged parental tome filled her voice. He became the "dumb" little brother. She seemed to enjoy her they

biting
would argue and then before I knew it back trying to fuck. He couldnt get it up. More out of coontrol

poking
Cigarettes and drinking. He hurt   emotionally too,   with anger. finally

sloppy kissingsmoking,drinking
he he so frustrated and taut he started slapping. A smile. She hit back.   More

hits   during it all calling each other Mommy and Daddy

I hid these pictures for years

O NOT CROSS

DAddy
Fucking Rhinda
ME

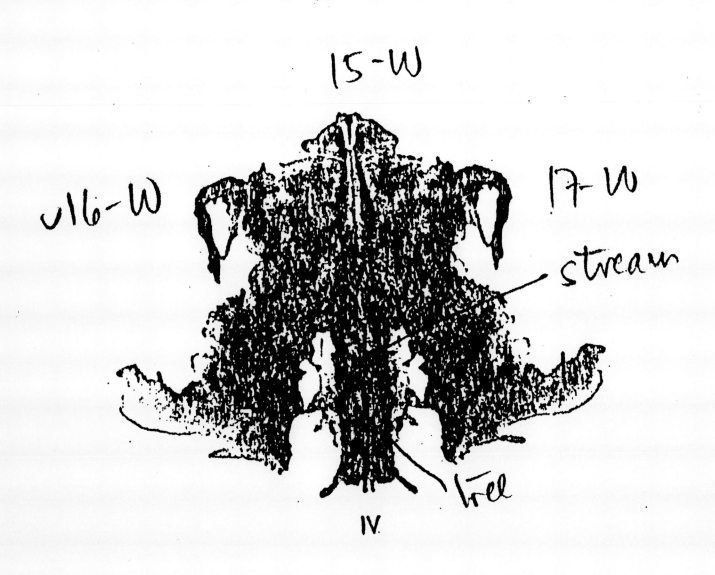

15-W

16-W

17-W

stream

tree

IV.

I Have 2 pairs of BLACK Jeans
"3   "2 turtlenecks
~~1 long sleeve oc/pc~~ Tee Shirt
· Long Sleeve AC/DC
2 pair of Shoes
& No Jacket !!! ☹
thats ALL   IS COLD in Hollycwood

San Francisco

Brandy, a.k.a. Stevie Kaos, is stuck in juvie until her grandmother can hire a lawyer to get her out. She had run from drug rehab and cracked up the new car that her family bought for her. Stevie was bingeing again, this time on crack and heroin. She married Demon, but he's in jail too. They were picked up for second degree robbery. A gun was involved. If she gets out and goes home she won't last long, since she wants to hitch to Miami to do some stripping.

YGC

I go to YGC, the San Francisco Youth Guidance Center. RAGE. Holes are punched through the wallboard. Tags cover every surface. Dirty underwear is all over the floor. YGC is obviously understaffed. An underpaid head counselor gives me a tour. He tells me that he's been working there for twenty years and loves his job.

> **Counselor:** Welcome to the home of murderers, five-thousand-buck-a-month crack-selling rapists. These are the motherfuckers who fucked their dads — then strangled their sisters — then robbed a bank — then killed a stranger. These are the cold blooded killing animals who can't be helped.

I photograph the open, empty rooms. When I walk by the locked cells, I see the kids inside. They act like they want to hurt me. With all their might they bang on the doors with fists and foreheads, yelling.

> **Kid #1:** What are you doing, mothafuckin' white boy? Get the fuck outta here. Your white momma is in here suckin' me off. Bend over and I'll fuck the shit out of you like I did to your daddy before her. Fuck you, mothafucka.
>
> **Kid #2:** Why is this white boy fuckin' filmin' here? Just like the Man to get me in here and show me as I is. If I ever get outta here I'm gonna get that camera and bust it up your ass.
>
> **Kid #3:** When I get outta here, I'm goin' to beat the shit outta you, Peppermint Breath.

The expert's opinion

> **Professional:** By and large, we are continuing to be over-run with kids who are in trouble, kids who have trouble growing up, kids who don't have a home to go to, or kids who are rebelling against a home that they don't like. Sometimes there's no sexual abuse, no alcoholism, maybe not even a divorce. But somehow the kid doesn't feel affiliated and gets to be 13 and boom, they run and run and run — to the thrill of being out on the street, the pull of that peer group — thinking that they're on top, that they're like Tarzan in their own jungle. After a while, they get into a little dealing or some hooking, and before you know it, they get into

the big time stuff. That's how the runaways enter into the juvenile system, wearing their rejection on their sleeves or carved into their arms.

You know, I'm the first to agree that the worst thing in the world is to be locked down, and yes, we must try to understand these kids. God knows they need it. But at some point we have to say fuck it. Some of these kids have defied and broken every natural law that has been written for their own, as well as the community's, protection.

Once in here we try to counsel them, "therapize" them, clothe them, and feed them. Our goal is to not let the young person out until they've proven to us that they can live in society without breaking the rules. But if they don't show something in the way of workable potential and they decide to be "dark angels" who make a lot of noise about "going out in a blaze of glory," we say fine, fuck them. They're not going to make it. We can't pull them out of the fire. So all we do is go through the motions 'til they're 18, let the adult system kick in, and then move them into the warehouses we build for the adult losers.

See, there are just too many kids and too few services to waste time on someone who keeps fucking up. So you put your energy into the cases that might have a successful outcome. Quite frankly, the possibility of getting a well-adjusted kid out of the system is pretty damn slim because then you have to send them home to the same inept parents who will never make it work. Maybe this is all happening because our young people are going downhill first before the rest of us. These kids are symbolic of our country's deterioration. Just look at our American family values. We are too selfish to have any values.

I recognize that I'm pessimistic, so maybe I'm not the guy you should be talking to. But in the thirteen years that I've been doing this work I've seen real qualitative changes. When I first started working in juvenile hall, we still had hubcap thieves. Now I see more and more kids who really have no regard for the value of life. And these kids are procreating and our problems are being magnified five or six times in their children. So you see, people in my business are not going to lose their jobs. This is a growth industry, good as the utility company.

So we either have to wait for them to kill each other off, or, if we want to be brave about it, we bite the bullet, take it on the chin, decide that we have to sacrifice two or three generations, and just concentrate on the kids being born today.

Jim: If you could do something, anything, what would you do?

Professional: I'd get in their face a lot.

As I leave YGC, I see lawyers in the lobby explaining bargaining rights to a 10 year old boy, when all he wants to do is make a paper airplane.

Springtime in Hollywood

Everything's the same — only worse. There are more police on the Boulevard now. Still, everything feels more dangerous. Weapons are hidden everywhere. Violence is part fashion, part necessity, in a world where there are few possibilities except for shit going up your arms and lives going down the drain. Napoleon is cruising the Boulevard carrying an ax, a hammer, and a screwdriver. He is not quite sure where he is since he just got out of detox and slammed a quarter of a gram.

Things change. The kids are having children of their own. Every other story I hear is about someone who has AIDS, who got beat up, or who is slamming too much dope. Still, there is a sense of hope among them that is beyond anything I can really comprehend.

Fame

We are hiding out inside the Fame Café. Bob Marley is singing "I Shot the Sheriff" on the jukebox. Someone is after Vyper, trying to shoot him down over a bunk dope deal. Vyper wants to show me a picture of his daughter, Hope, but he lost it. He is nodding out, looking like he'll OD at any moment. He gives me his tattoo machine, his mom's phone number, and all his drawings and says he won't be needing them any more.

I call Vyper's mom to warn her about his slow suicide mission, telling her straight-up that he won't make it. She knows this already. She asks if I remember Tyler, who is now HIV positive. He and Vyper have always shared needles and Vyper refuses to get tested. Besides, he is screwing everyone in sight. She asks for my advice. I am stymied because she is an obviously loving parent, the director of a children's agency, a therapist, and social worker. She has spent tens of thousands of dollars trying to help him, "trying everything and anything." She tells me that after a certain point there is nothing you can do, that he is like a tortured animal in a cell, pacing back and forth, waiting to be released. Sometimes she wishes it would all be over. It would be a relief for her and for him, a release from his internal hell.

Youth shelter

Dave is staying with Ian, the ex-sugardaddy turned street worker. Ian is crazy as ever, bringing new kids to the Lido, a dark hellhole with a broken elevator, a stained carpet, and boarded up windows, where they stay 'til they get sick of him or each other or the TV. Ian says he is trying to raise money to buy a van for his "youth foundation." His "shelter" is a one room mess with a bunk bed, a mattress, and a TV/VCR on the floor. The closet has piles of dirty clothes pouring out of it.

Dave has long, bleached hair and only two teeth left. He's watching a vampire movie with Casper and Mia. They've seen it fifty seven times. Casper likes to freebase and

gang bang. She shows us her tattoos and how to "de-virginize" a teddy bear. She is sucking on a pacifier. Mia, 16, used to be a model and has plans to become one again. She ran away from home last week. She already misses shopping with her mom and her braces are hurting her. She's wondering whether or not to call her orthodontist. Mia is proud of her virginity and emphasizes that she'll remain a virgin until she marries Vamp-child, a cute boy she just met who says he's a real vampire. She didn't believe him at first but then noticed that she couldn't see him in the mirror at McDonald's. He took her out back of the Oasis and she saw him draw blood from this bum who then disappeared.

June, Greco's Pizza

Dave: We're all in the gutter but some of us can see the stars better than others.

Jim: Where's Ziggy?

Dave: Ziggy is living off whores. And the whores live off the sugardaddies. And they all have AIDS. Ziggy thinks he might have AIDS. Me too. Look at my teeth. One falls out every time I brush them or suck somebody's dick. Speaking of whores, how's Echo doin'? Does she have AIDS? I don't even remember what she looks like.

Jim: She's three months pregnant, Dave.

Dave: Damn. I certainly didn't do it, although I think she'd fuck me under the right circumstances. Was it that asshole, Doug?

Jim: She thinks so but she's not really sure.

Dave: I'll kill the mothafucka if he don't take care of her. You know, if Echo wanted me I'd do anything for her, anything. Even live. 'Cause I'm getting really sick, dude. Fevers and all these weird pains.

Jim: Are you going to a doctor?

Dave: Maybe tomorrow or Tuesday.

Later, Hollywood Boulevard

Everyone is threatening to kill somebody.

Vampchild: Vyper and the Crossfire Skins invaded Rag Doll's squat, going ape shit at three a.m. They beat up Mexican Gustaf, stole his boots, held a knife to me, and then kidnapped and raped Mia. I had no choice.

Rag Doll: I was too fucked-up in bed when it was all goin' down. But either way, the Crossfire Skins wouldn't ever try to start no shit with me. All I saw was Crow pulling out his knife and saying, "Mia's goin' with me." Vampchild didn't do shit about it 'cause Vampchild ain't worth shit.

Tori: I heard that the Crossfire Skins raped Mia, but I'm not sure if that's true because Vyper wouldn't ever do nothin' like that. Plus, I saw Mia this morning and she was stoned. Either way, I gave her the number of the counselor at the crisis center where I went when I was raped.

Perry: I saw Mia a couple of hours ago, crying, trying to find a knife 'cause she wanted to kill herself. I'm positive that she got raped, especially if L. Boy, Crow, Vyper, Dominic, and the two Steves were involved. They're the kind of people who give kids a bad name. I'd kill the motherfuckers if I was Vampchild.

Mia is sitting on Vampchild's lap, giving him hickeys and using all this attention to prove that she's tough.

Mia: You can poke holes in me, even make fun of me, and I won't cry. My little girl is hidden deep inside.

Gustaf's face is a mess. He thinks the reason this all happened is because Satan put a "rape spell" on Mia. Gustaf tried to break the spell by levitating her, but it didn't work. For him it proves that Satan is stronger and will kill him.

Gustaf: I swear I'm not Mexican and gay like the Crossfire Skins said.
I'm a full-blooded German white boy whose mom and dad believe in Hitler and are Satanists. It's like this: my parents put this spell on me, see. When I was growing up, there were all these fucking incredible rituals. Chanting, killing animals, drinking blood, eating flesh. They made me do all this shit. They said, "do it or die." They even cut a baby into little pieces and spread the blood and guts over my body. Then I had to fuck my mother while she licked my body, and dude, ever since, I have these, like, cravings for blood and a desire to be the beast.

Heather is a 15 year old blond rich kid who left her prep school life, stole her mom and dad's car and credit cards, started running, and hasn't stopped since. She is pregnant with twins and tries to comfort Gustaf.

Heather: Jesus will save you eventually. Do you want some Cheerios?

Gustaf, mourning the loss of his boots, walks barefoot toward Santa Monica Boulevard to hustle up some comfort. This is the end of Hollywood for me.

Polk Street, San Francisco

Marcos is with Will, his 15 year old boyfriend. They've been together for almost a year. They say they've been tweeked for two days, ever since Marcos got out of jail, where he was sent for assaulting a cop. Their eyes are painfully red. The two are barking at each other about whether or not Marcos treats Will like a child or if Will acts like one. Will argues that if Marcos sends him out to get a pack of cigs, then it's Marcos's fault if Will doesn't come back 'til four in the morning, totally geeked.

Marcos looks different, even good from far away, like an older, more professional whore. His hair is delicately styled and his beard seems neatly manicured. Upon closer examination, one can detect the obvious flaws in his style. He's dressed in layers and the stained clothes are the same ones I had seen on him weeks ago. His empty pockets are ripped at the seams. He has a plastic bag with a toothbrush, some toiletries, and maybe some underwear. He looks like he slept on his face and now his hand is broken, so he can't snap his fingers like he used to. They need a ride to get a window fixed 'cause Marcos threw Will through it.

Marcos and Will keep breaking up but they always seem to find each other again. They fence TVs, stereos, jewelry, anything, for drugs and the "thousands" that they owe everybody else. Will has begun pulling dates on Polk Street and he enjoys it. All his money is spent on speed, which he smokes in a glass pipe. He is not careful with tricks. Marcos doesn't care either because he uses dirty needles.

> **Marcos:** Girl, it's not the first stupid thing I've done. Shit, Jim, I haven't been tested yet, but I feel like I got it 'cause Troy's got it. And Troy's ex-boyfriend died of it and Troy and Will never had safe sex but.... Who knows, maybe it's only staph.... But I figure I don't care, 'cause then I'll have something to live and die for, 'cause child....

He tries to sing some line from a jukebox song:

> **Marcos:** If that's what it takes to find love, then I'll risk my life for him....

Meanwhile, Will sees a potential date and thinks $100 bills. He gets in the truck and drives off with the date. Marcos confides in me that he wishes he could decide between Will and Brad.

Will comes back beaming, sucking on a popsicle. He flashes keys to a hotel room that the john got him for a week. Marcos quickly makes dream plans to get a phone in the room with voice mail, so they can sell speed and then buy a van and then.... Marcos continues mumbling some diatribe to himself — about drugs and how all his old friends are either in jail or dead, and how the straight world just doesn't understand how together he is. As they leave, Marcos's voice gets louder and louder, screaming that he's going to kill Deion because he owes him money, and fading and fading off into a....

> **Marcos:** I need to get high so I can handle the stress of my welfare appointment tomorrow, girl!

Sean, Portland

Sean calls from a rest stop near Portland. He has become Tank again and has just woken up drunk in the back of a pick-up on his way to Colorado, looking for some girl he met in court who he thinks he loves. He wishes me "peace" and says that he's happy because some woman wants to pay him a lot of money to write a book about his life.

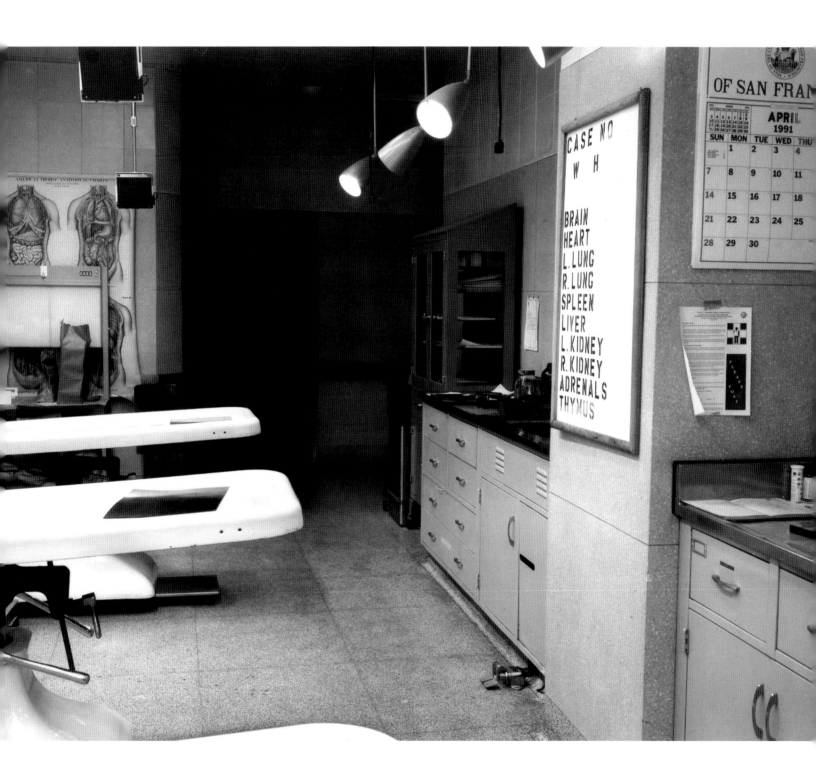

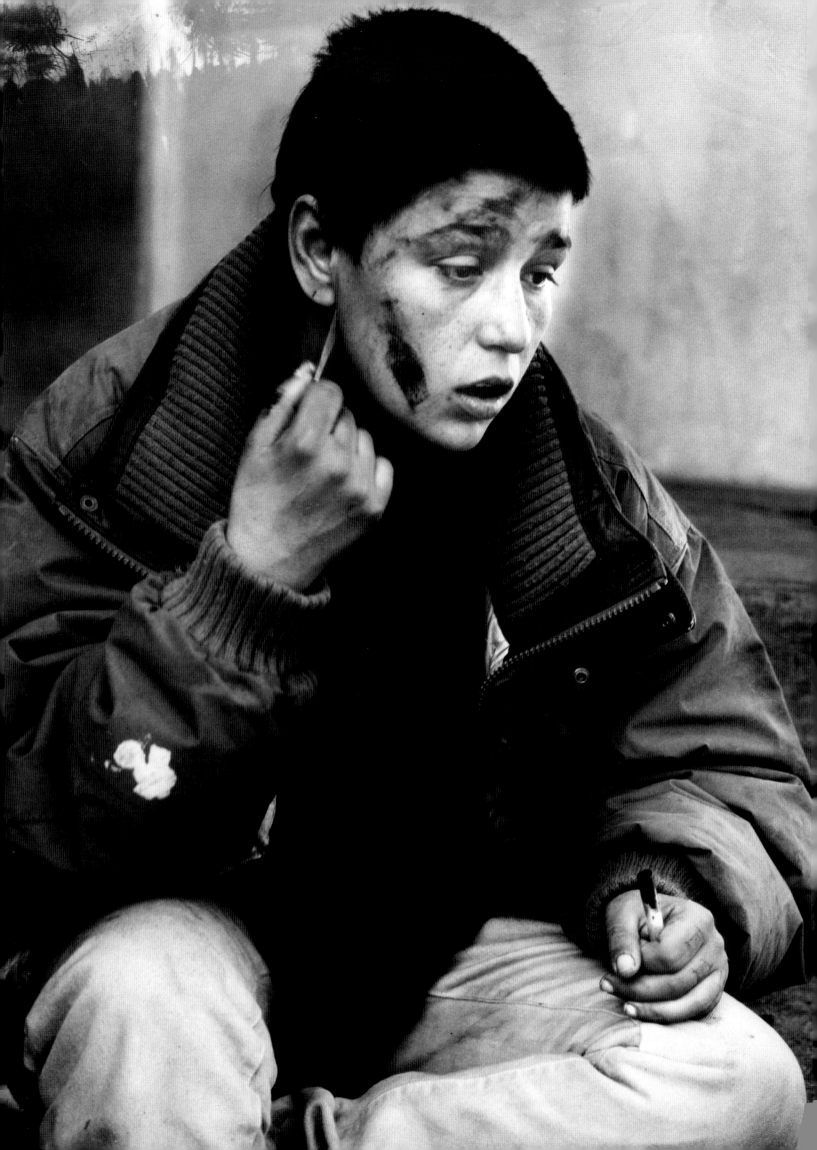

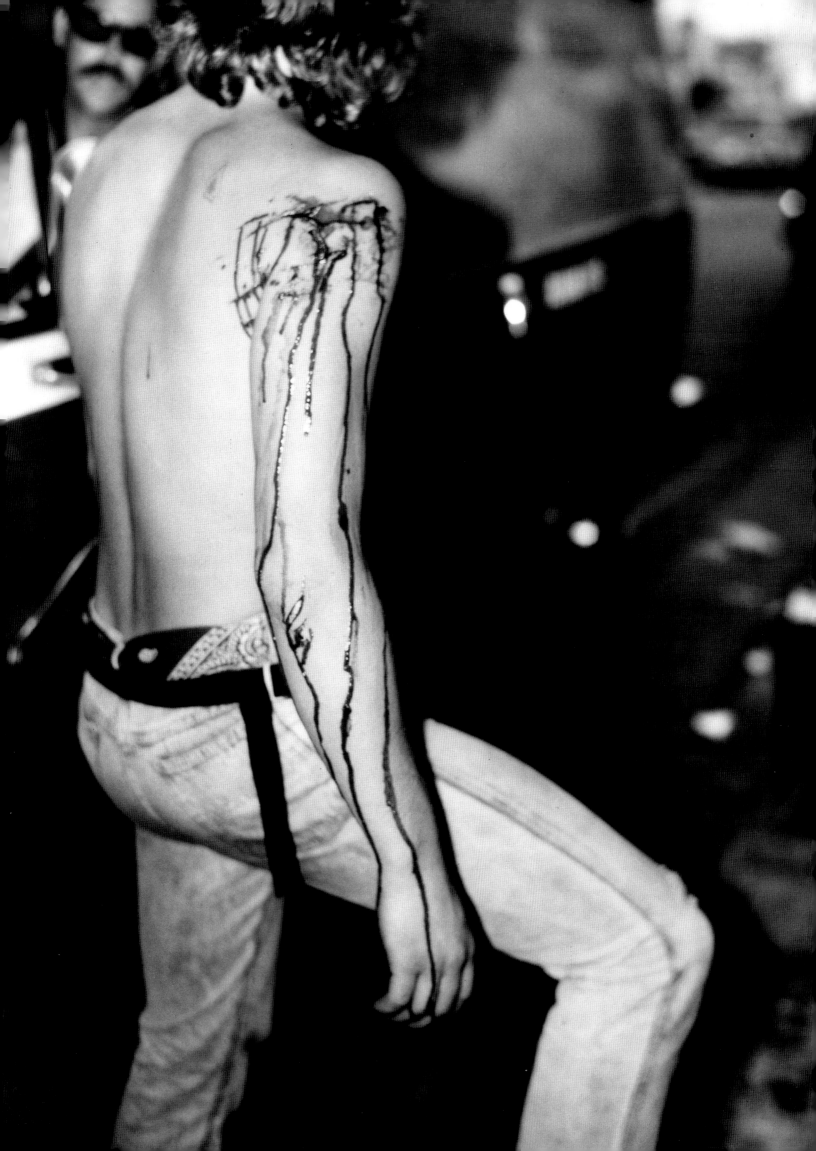

I like looking like MADONNA

I feel like shit.

HOLLYWOOD TINA XMAS

UNIVER...

NO LOITERING

WE RESERVE THE RIGHT TO REFUSE SERVICE TO ANYONE

NOT RESPONSIBLE FOR ARTICLES LEFT HERE

REST... FOR ... UN...

To the rest of the world FUCK you.

I love Hollywood Stoners

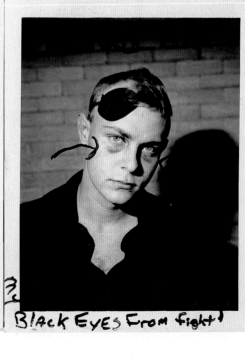

BLACK EYES from fight

Psycho-Bitch
Psycho
Dusty
Rusty
Robert
Riff Raff
Jane
Tarzan
Tree
Black Pops
Wes
Mad Max
Little One
Lil' Bit
B.J.
Napoleon
Sarah
Theresa
Clone
Destroyer
Molly
Micki
Bunny
Gonnorhea Donna (Porno Donna)
Stressful Lisa
Tamra
Alex
N.Y. Steve
Yankee
rebel
mama bear
Prankster (Rick)
Zip code
m + m
Scat
Fuckhead
Puke
Vomit
Trasher
dog

preacher
Kelly
Ice
Mia
Jersey Sue
Heather
Baby Crazy
Sid
Nancy
Nightmare
Cruise
Stewart
Casper
Skater Mike
Skateboard Dave
Skin head Josh
Brian
Crystal
Cupid
Kato
Brian
J How
Drunk Michelle
Fastey
Sunshine
Stinky
Hot Dog
Cheerio
Red
Blackie
Lupa
Tartak
Albert
Cutter
Shaeffer
Heavy Flavor
Dominic
Spirit
Free Bird

Wasted
Bandit
Macki
Monique
Tabitha
Bam Bam
Reckless
Delphi
Romeo
Poison
Wall
Wino Ron
Rex
Borg
Kami
Tisha
Mishta
Napoleon
Cat Eyes
Stresser
Perry
Nick the Dick
Gazebo
Rose
Blamm
Doc
Destiny
Louis
Tweety Wes
Diamond
Crazy
Damn
Damien
Fuck
Eagle
Frenchy
Ozzie
Lace
Fucked up Lisa

Looking tough

Wayne

RAGDOLL Just got off the bus (homeless)
CURB CREW
DORCC →
Hollywood Blvd

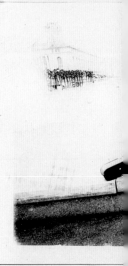

Jim
I THINK I'M
GONNA CUT
THIS OFF
THANX FOR
SAYING "THE
PICTURE'S
GOING TO
TURN OUT
GREAT."
LUV
XOXO
WE

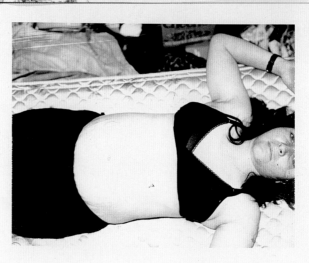

Aaron

CHRIS

GREETINGS FROM Hollywood

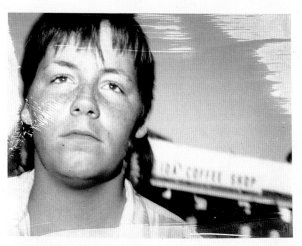

SCOTT

CASE NO
W H

BRAIN
HEART
L. LUNG
R. LUNG
SPLEEN
LIVER
L. KIDNEY
R. KIDNEY
ADRENALS
THYMUS

I am a norm a. L PERSON

looking at

so what the Hell are you

scott
and drunk

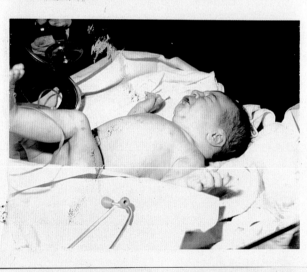

changla is a
dope head.

CRON
DRUNK

HRP

FUCK THE
WORLD!

eh? I ain't

Done nothing wrong yet!

L.Lilik

HOLLYWOOD

KFW

XAVIER

Corona

AXE
AXEL
I DON'T KNOW
BOMBER
JUNKIE
DOPER
DOPEY
DOPER Molly
MEDEA
MARCOS
VYPER
D-ONE
BRUISER
NIKY
NIKKI
SKID
FREAK
HARLEY MIKE
HARLEY DAVE
BIKER Jerry
Thomas The Pimp
PUKEFACE
ABCE
J.D.
ANNE-MARIE
CHAOS
KAOS
MOOSE
COUGAR
Panther
CHIEF
Magik
Fry Boy
Melissa
Nikki Pain
CHUCO
Carlos
MARCOS
LEE
BRAD
SPIKE

VELVET
SID #2
WINTER
Summer
SPRING
SPRUNG
TORI
DEBORAH Morning-Owl
OUTLAW
GUSTAF
STRIDER
SAD MAN
STONER CHRIS
SKATER CHRIS
STONEY BETH
DRUNK MELANIE
SHILOH
SHA
SHY BOY
HOMEGROWN
Baby-CRAZY
Baby LOCA
TROUBLE
WICKED
SATAN
DEVIL
DEMON WOLF
DEMON
WOLF
WOLFETTE
RICOCHET
Baby girl
DOC T
OLD MAN DOG
OLD MAN PAT
SICK RICK
TROUBLE CHILD (T.C.)
THC
DUST
BREEZE

CYNTHIA
CHRISSIE
~~crossed out~~
Johnnie -AKA- TWALK Jack
NATHAN
JEANNETTE
LOUIS
MISCHIEF
STEPHANIE
MICKEY
TAMRA
SABRINA
THERESA
MELODY
NICKI CHAOS
BASEL
TOM
HEAVEN
HELL
IGGY
China Blue
Blue
Black
Fuck up
Fry Boy
CRY Baby
SIS
SISSY
COMA
SCRATCH
Scarface Rob
Doug
POPCORN
ISIS
Baby Face Rob
Little Michael
Antoine
Sampson
Sambo

NYC
Xmen #
Schaffer

MAX
This is #57
A Bad
Bu Picture
Because
I Am
To Happy

POLAROID ® R802431R

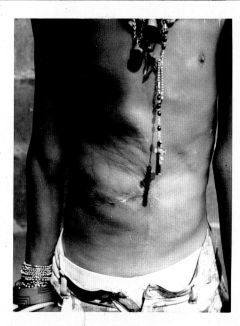

Good luck
in life,
Bobby

Lil' mac
KOF

R×I×P
Fo×-Be×
HK
CU₹₹₹

Full Slabs

ROBERT FOWLKES — 21 1988
ARLEY

I'M A MENTAL DISTURB.
I' WAS CHILD MOLESTED.
THEY CHOKES ME AND BEAT. ME.
THEY PLAY WITH MY PEENIS.
I' HAVE PROBLEM WITH PEEOPLE.
I'M NOT NORMAL KID.
SOMETIME i FEEL LIKE.
A LITTEL KID IN A BIG BODY.
I' LIKE TO BLOW UP THE WORLD.
I WANT TO GET MY OWN WAY.
DONT WANT TO LISSTEN.
TO NOBODY.
MY MOM AND DAD REEJECT. ME
THEY TOOK A HAMMER TOO MY. LEG.
AND BEATED ME — BRAIAN DAMAGE.
THERE IS NO LOVE IN MY LIFE.
THINGS ARE ALL WRONG.
I SUCK DICK FOR $$$
THERE IS NO CHRISTMAS FOR ME (IN 88)
MAYBE THIS YEAR i GROW UP AND GET.
MARRIED AND HAVE THREEE KIDS.
I HOPE i HAVE MY LIFE TOGETHER

Mickey and the baby, San Francisco

Mickey is now 19. Two years ago she bottomed out. She was tired of being Blade, tired of Tank, tired of the needles and the same ol' scam of it all. She ended up in New Hampshire in a rural residency treatment program with her new boyfriend Jeff, full of hope. Periodically she called to let me know how long she had been clean. She loved to talk about her garden, the animals on the nearby farms, the counseling, and about getting better. Eventually she and Jeff got their own apartment with a phone and it all sounded great. I had no reason to doubt her story or her desire to make her life better, since she had taken advantage of everything the system had to offer. She was one of the few success stories that I knew. Then she got pregnant and moved back to California to live with Jeff and the baby at his parent's house.

Mickey calls me collect.

> **Mickey:** I ran away from Jeff's mom's house with the baby. And I can't go back, Jim. His mom is all pissed at me 'cause I called the cops on him after he hit me. I couldn't be myself there. See, he was doin' a gun trade and brought home two pounds of speed. And I gave in and slammed. And I knew right away I had to get out, that I couldn't have my baby around all this.
>
> Right now, I'm in southern California at my uncle and aunt's house. He's a paranoid schizo who's always looking through his own garbage and she's this cum-guzzlin' alcoholic who drinks whole bottles of peppermint schnapps in one sitting. And damn if they don't fight a lot. They say they will give me money if I promise to leave the baby with them. I'm thinking of giving them custody because, as I see it, I have no choice and I can't handle the stress no more. I'm confused and don't know what to do. I'm getting so angry at the kid and I don't want to do to her what my mom and dad did to me. I'm so tired of mothering. I want to go dancing. I want to get laid. I want to go to Colorado and take some parenting classes and join a gym and lift weights.

A few days later, Jeff drives down to southern California. He picks up Mickey and the baby from her uncle and aunt's house and drives back up to San Francisco. He takes the baby and leaves Mickey on our doorstep.

> **Mickey:** I'm too young to have a child. Jeff doesn't want to fuck me anymore 'cause I'm too fat and anyway, he says he's found somebody better. I decided the baby should go with him. Maybe he can handle it all better than me 'cause I'm asking myself now, "Hey, why not do speed, get high, pull a few tricks, get a hotel room, get set up?"

She tells us about last night, when they were driving up here in the car and the baby was screaming and screaming and screaming.

Mickey: We both start getting frustrated and Jeff starts speeding. And by this time the baby is sitting on my lap, still screaming, and I yell at Jeff not to speed. The baby continues to scream and then Jeff goes like he's gonna hit her and I go, "Jeff, just calm down, be patient. She's just tired or has gas and is nervous." And Jeff's like, "Okay." And he calms down. And then the baby goes to sleep. Then Jeff's all sweet and nice to me, promising me this and promising me that. But I don't know anymore, since maybe he wasn't sober. And now I'm thinking that maybe it was a mistake to have left the baby with him.

We decide to put Mickey up in a hotel and help her begin to make various contacts with the agencies, to find shelter, figure out her options about what to do and what's right for the baby. One shelter won't accept her because she used needles in the past. Another program won't because the baby's too old. Another won't because the baby's too young. Most shelters are full — beyond overloaded — and ask her to call back tomorrow, or better yet, in three weeks.

The phone call

Mickey: Okay, I'll spell it out for you. C-A-R-N-E-Y. Um, nope. White. Uh. No, um, in the past four months? New Hampshire to California to Colorado, then back to here…. My last permanent address? Um, dee dum, dum, it was 1847 Payne Way. P-A-Y-N-E. In Colorado. No. Yes. I stayed there with a friend until I had to move out because she couldn't handle the baby crying and things like that. I was in New Hampshire for two years in drug treatment. Yes, with my boyfriend. No. We just recently broke up. No. Yes. He doesn't have a job. Uh, huh. I stayed with my aunt and I called social services there and told them I felt I was incapable of taking care of the child and that….

Um, I, um, I didn't want to give my daughter up because, well, because I've been in the system, in and out of foster homes since I was like 7, and…. No, I wouldn't. Sure. Yes, he hit me. In the back of the head. I blacked out. Uh, um. No. He's not going to come and get me. It's nothing like that. He's got the baby, so he has no reason to come looking for me. Yes, I'm positive. I'd stake my life on it. Right now? I'm at a friend's house and I just need to talk to someone and get a place to stay so I can think and not go nuts and not use drugs because….

Uh huh. Well, I was using speed on a daily basis since I was 13. Yes, detox. In New Hampshire. Yes, I was clean for twenty three months. Yes, speed. Yes, I used bleach. Um, no. Six weeks ago. No, I'm not. Um, three shots of vodka. Yes. Huh?

Um, yes. They still have my case on file. It's called the Boulder Safe House. Yes, I had the child with me. No. Yeah, but, uh, yes, as far as hitting me when I was pregnant, yes that's true. But it's not all his fault. His name? Jeff Phillips. Um, yes, he twelve-stepped with me. Uh, he claims that he's not, but, you know, he's always playing with my head. No. Yes. No. I figured. I hope not. That's why I need to talk to someone about my child.

See, I've got a plane ticket to go to Colorado. Yes, that's right, but maybe I should stay in San Francisco, or maybe go back to New Hampshire. No. I don't want to. She's not safe with me. I mean, I have no patience. Yes. I'm afraid of shaking the baby. I just need some guidance in my life. No. What? We got a court date for a custody hearing. I mean, I want this child. I mean, if I can keep her and, you know. Okay. No, I haven't filed here. How come? What? I was told I didn't have to. No. What? What's that? I mean, wait. No. NO!

Mickey hangs up on the "bitch" who put her on hold.

Mickey: Fuck 'em. I don't have no time to wait for them. I'm fucking going to Colorado and leaving the baby with Jeff 'cause it's too hard and hectic and I can't cope. Fuck it!

Mickey's story is never the same. She changes it depending on who she's talking to. By now I don't know what's true or not. I find it's getting harder to trust her, even though I want to believe her. The next day Mickey takes the bus to Jeff's mom's house, hoping things will work out. Just as abruptly she returns the following afternoon to San Francisco with the child.

The baby trusts no one. She is limp. When we pick her up she tenses, arches her back. There's not much life in her eyes either. Just a bit of hope for future comfort. Mickey and the baby watch cartoons all day. Mickey says it's to shut them both up. The baby cries a lot. All the baby wants is to be picked up, comforted, and have her diaper changed.

Susan finds Mickey in the middle of the night, exasperated, crying, and yelling violently at her 3 month old girl, pressing the baby's hands down on the bed, force feeding her to try to get her to sleep. In the morning Mickey decides that she's ready to learn to be a parent. In the afternoon she speaks to Jeff on the phone and wants to return to his mom's house. It's inconceivable to me that she could go back to him now. It's like choosing death over life. I don't try to hide my angry disappointment. After all, Jeff's life hasn't been much better than Mickey's.

Mickey: His father would molest him, then take him to a whorehouse where they would fuck the same girl.

Jim: Don't go with him.

Mickey: I give up. What are my choices?

Jim: There are more phone calls to be made.

Mickey: I just want to go with Jeff and make it better. I just want to go numb.

Jeff arrives at our house and the first thing he does is yell at the baby for crying. Mickey quiets him, embarrassed by his bad behavior. They leave. I compare this to the alternative. Our own daughter smiles. She has books, toys, and trust. Unconditional love. Susan is crying, telling me we are helpless. I hurt so bad I want to believe that this problem will just go away, so I can feel comfortable again and get on with my life. I can't look at Mickey and Jeff and believe that their kid will be fine. Instinct and my limited understanding of psychology hint that the baby won't make it.

I want answers, now. I want to save this baby. I am filled with sadness, shock, rage. This is no Hollywood movie fairy tale. I can't walk away after the lights go up. With each unyielding interaction with Mickey or the system, I get that "I can't do shit" kind of feeling. But none of this talk will save Mickey's kid. I want to make more phone calls and help them however I can, but Mickey, Jeff, and the baby disappear without an address or number.

Later

Out of the blue, Mickey calls. She's in Colorado, on her way to New Hampshire, and she's pregnant again.

> **Mickey:** Jeff's in jail for threatening to kill me. The baby's in a foster home. My life is a mess and, as usual, I caused it. I'm thinking about having an abortion. Jeff told me he didn't love me and he didn't want me or the baby and that he was an alcoholic. I need to take more responsibility for myself. That's why I'm leaving in an hour. Got to go. Love you. Bye, Jim.

Mickey calls again. She's back in New Hampshire with her first child, and she now has another baby girl who she named Darling. Jeff's in a New Hampshire jail for three counts of domestic assault, two counts of unlawful mischief, one count of simple assault, one count of unlawful trespass, and one of aggravated assault. Mickey says he might get out in five to ten and she's going to wait for him.

> **Mickey:** He went on a five hour spree. He hit me five times in the back of the head and bashed me in the face. He was drunk and on sleeping pills and stabbed a guy in the back of the neck with a pair of scissors.

Speaking to her a few days later, Mickey says it's fifteen to twenty years for Jeff. She told him that she wasn't going to wait for him. She's going to do nude modeling for $20 an hour. On Friday she had a relapse: drinking, a line of coke, a hit of pot. She says she's okay now because she has three counseling appointments and two parenting classes next week.

> **Mickey:** Jim, hell and evil live within all of us. The reason I exist is to let normal people feel better about who they are. This way they won't have to deal with what's fucked-up inside themselves or the world. And they can always blame us kids: the Mickeys, the Jeffs, or the Tanks.

I am worried about Mickey's two daughters. I try to call the Department of Social Services in New Hampshire to ask for help.

> **Case worker:** I'm very sorry, Mr. Goldberg, but you're asking the government to get involved in the personal life of one of our clients without proof of anything.

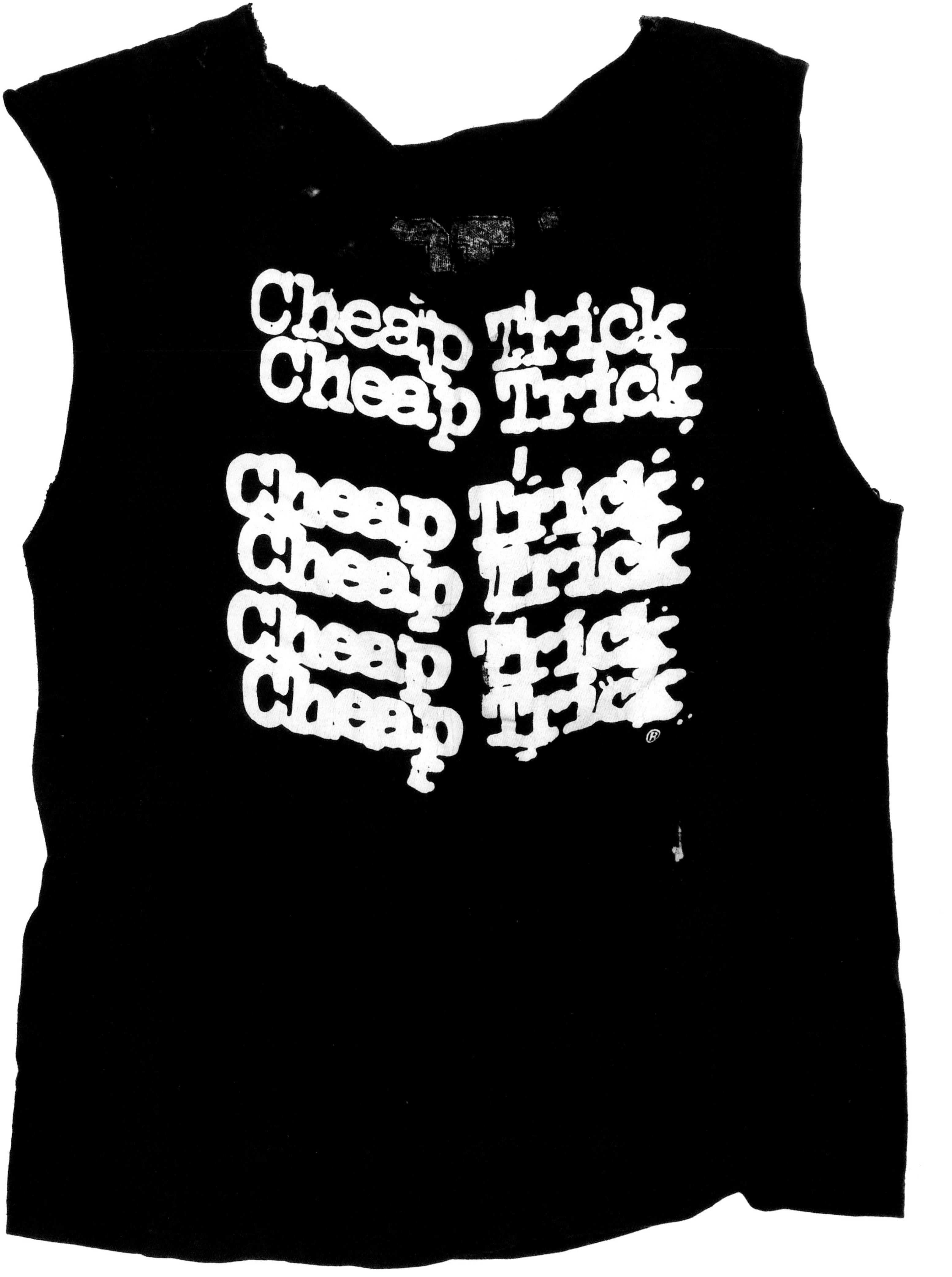

September, Room 32, Crystal Hotel, San Francisco

Echo has been off tweek for over three months, a hundred and one days exactly. She is now six months pregnant and is due around Christmas. She claims to be happy for the first time in memory. Her mom is even coming out for the birth. She has long since given up on Doug. He was a loser anyway and caused her too much pain, beating her and throwing her down the stairs.

Her new boyfriend Johnny, a.k.a. Twack Jack, is a dog-faced-surfer-geek who uses big words wrong. Echo and Johnny are dealing speed out of their room. There is a continuous flow, in and out, of people buying drugs. Usually there is one or two guys, sitting, standing, and rambling into discombobulated stories, mostly about drugs. Someone is always tweeking on the contents of their wallet, grinding a kitchen knife into a weapon, or shooting up in the bathroom. In one corner there are piles of garbage bags filled with clothes for Echo's baby. Each item has a story behind it, about which dumpster it was found in, or which friend gave it to Echo because they had lost their own kids, taken away by the welfare people because of the drugs.

The birth of Amber, San Francisco

It's the week before Christmas. Dave has been calling collect every day to find out "when the bitch is going to drop." Echo's mom, R. Sylvia, arrives and she is staying with Susan and I until she takes Echo and her baby home to the suburbs. We are outside the Crystal Hotel and I imagine seeing it for the first time through R. Sylvia's eyes: there is a grim metal gate and a sign on tape that reads, "Ring Here." The switch for the bell consists of two wires that need to be placed together. It doesn't work. The door behind the gate is open and a huge man is sitting inside "sharing" a Polish Dog with a man who is crashed on the stairs above, too loaded to eat. The huge man sees us and, with mustard hands, opens the gate.

> **Man:** What's up? I'm the guard. You gotta picture ID?
>
> **Jim:** Room 32, Echo.

This reply gets us in. We ascend over the crashed out man to the second floor landing, where two little boys are playing football in the hall. Up another flight, two people are rummaging through the garbage. The door to Room 32 is partially busted in. Echo is asleep on a pile of clothes. Twack Jack is dressed, as always, like someone much younger than himself, a surfer with a bike, which he's tweekin' on.

> **Twack Jack:** You're Echo's mom? I'm real happy to meet you. I just got out of jail and I'm, like, like nervous, so I got to go out and catch some freedom. Hope you understand.

He splits to go for a bike ride. Another guy, Paul, is pressed into a chair in the corner, open sores on his body, counting money. He puts singles into groups of twenty. A girl, Bridget comes out of the bathroom biting her lips, geeked, with her hand across her arm, blood there. Echo wakes up. I head for home, leaving R. Sylvia to help Echo get organized and do laundry. Later that night R. Sylvia returns to our home.

> **R. Sylvia:** In their room there was dirty laundry everywhere. I looked in a corner and there was a curtain and I thought maybe there were books behind it or something, so I picked it up and there was more laundry. I figured that's how they decorated their room. They told me that they kept buying clothes for months and never quite got around to sorting them. I helped Beth do the laundry. There aren't any cabs in that neighborhood, so we carried sixteen bags to the laundromat. Beth has no idea how to operate a dryer. She doesn't know that you have to turn the thing and put a quarter in. But she did try to fold. We talked some. I find it very hard to know what to say to her after so long.
>
> I remember the last time I saw her was three years ago with Dave. I was out here trying to bring her home and Beth had this book she wanted me to read. It was called I Don't Want to Live this Life Anymore. I read it on the plane and I thought, "Oh my god." Beth really must have thought of herself as this person,

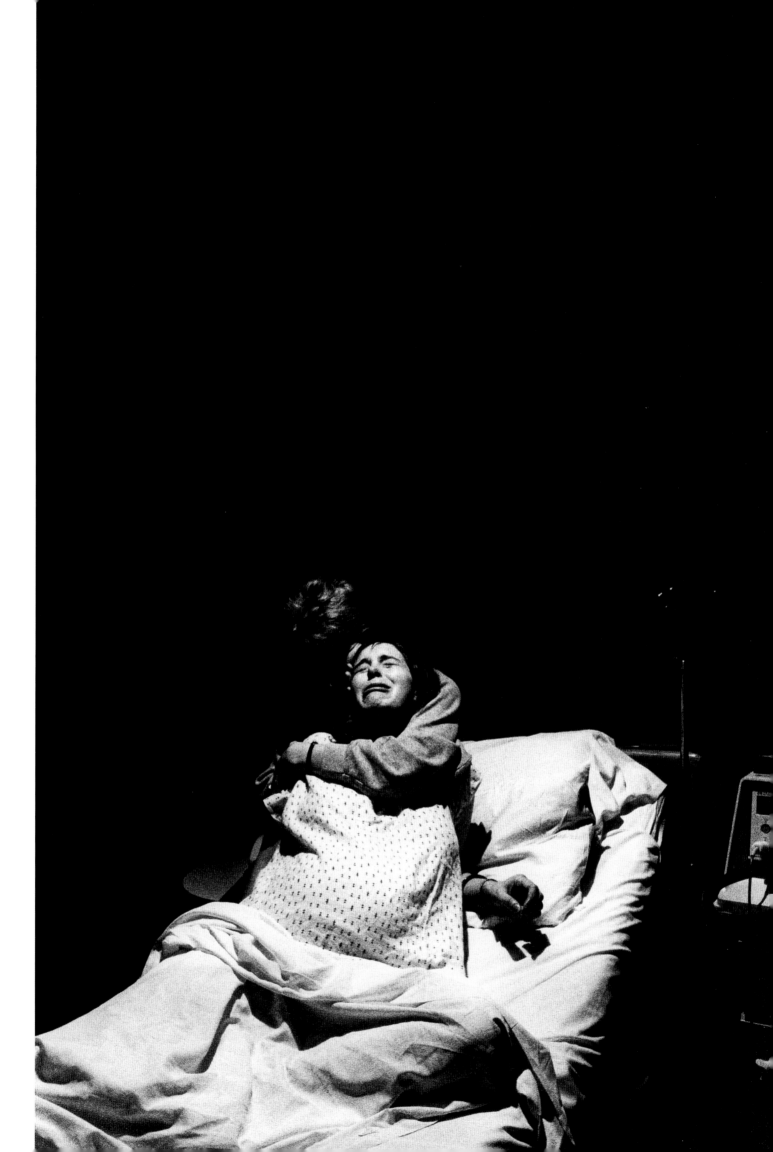

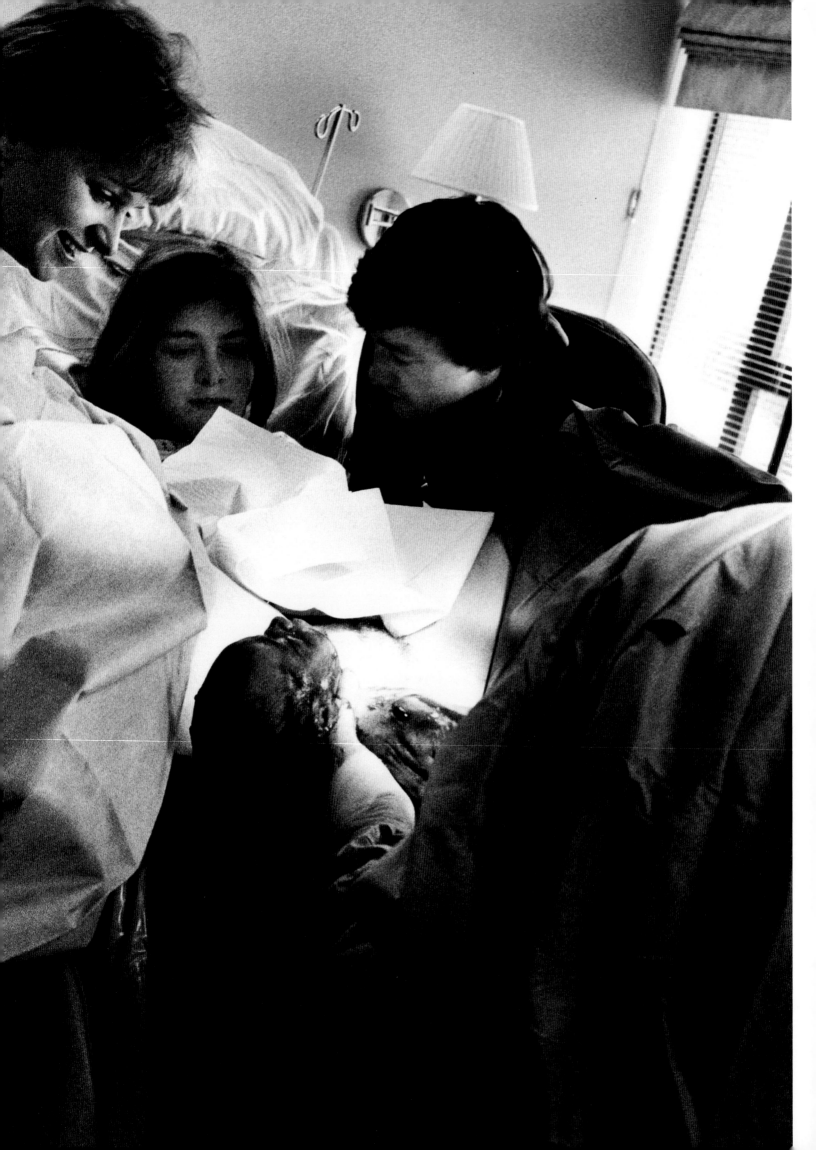

Nancy, waiting to die with her guy, Sid. It was then that I realized she was into it so deep that she may never get out.

Yesterday I asked her, "Why did you leave home and have to do all this stuff during these past five years?" Beth said, "I didn't want to come home, mom. At least not until I'd made something of myself." I asked her, "How can you make something of yourself in this situation?" She said, "Now I'm ready to come home."

I stopped there and knew not to push it. This is a fragile alliance that needs to be nurtured. I sometimes wonder what it would be like to have a normal daughter, one who only talks about decorating the nursery and shopping in malls, but I don't care anymore. She seems so happy. Except for him, Johnny. I don't think he helps. He certainly wasn't there to help do the laundry. He said he didn't feel well, that he was tired and feeling stressed. I could show him what stress is really about.

Part of me wants to tell R. Sylvia that Echo is still dealing, Paul is counting drug money, Bridget is four months pregnant, those dumpster diving people are all her daughter's friends, and bringing Echo and the baby home with her might not work. Then the phone rings.

Jim: Hello? Hey, what's up? Yeah, except I got Echo's mom here. Okay, later.

R. Sylvia: Who's that?

Jim: It's this guy, Tank. He wants to come over to get some money. I'm going to have to tell him off.

R. Sylvia: Johnny is not much better. I've seen how he manipulates Beth, gets her to take care of him. She'll go out to get him a candy bar, like he's helpless or something. Then she gets resentful and yells at him so much that she loses her voice. I'm determined to do anything to make it easier for Beth to come home. She says she loves him, so, against my better judgment, I have agreed to let him return with us. In my heart, I wish Twack Jack and all these people were locked away or dead.

I decide it's time to show R. Sylvia the dummy for the book I am working on about runaways. She goes through the pictures, page by page.

R. Sylvia: These kids have been beaten since the day they were born. You wonder if there's anything good they can draw on, hold on to, or come back to, so they can have a normal life. Most of them have really cold eyes, guns in their hands, or dope in their heads. They are a plague on society. They're a threat to everything that you and I hold important in our lives.

I think I wouldn't care, actually. I wish that they would just kill themselves off and go away. This is the only way to solve this problem. But then when I look at your pictures, Jim, I remember that my kid is in them. I mean, Beth has become someone who I don't want to look at. I don't think I can do anything about this situation, so I don't want to see it. I mean, if this could happen in my house, it could happen in anybody's house in America.

Amber, December 17, 10:35 a.m.

Echo is in labor. At two a.m., R. Sylvia and I drive to the Crystal Hotel where we find Twack Jack geeked on his bike, popping wheelies and trying to jump over garbage cans. His arms are flailing and he's howling repeatedly:

Twack Jack: I'm going to be a dad, I'm going to be a dad.

Upstairs in Room 32 Echo is ready. Paul is there "taking care" of her. Actually, he's been tweeking on Echo's hospital bag, packing it for the past two days. It contains a knife, four comic books, some insane writing, a pot pipe with a couple of hits, three packs of Marlboro 100s, a teddy bear, and a picture I took of Echo. Twack Jack refuses to leave his bike in the hotel room. Everyone but Paul piles into my car with the bike. Never having driven a woman in labor to the hospital, I'm driving way too fast and I can't see a thing with the bike in the back. I imagine being pulled over by a cop and watching a spun Twack Jack try to talk the cop into offering an escort to the hospital — with sirens and lights — like in some absurd movie. We arrive without incident and I drop them all off and park. I find Bridget in the pale yellow plastic waiting area of the hospital.

Bridget: I just slammed a half a gram of speed. Fucked this guy super hard. But the asshole hit me. Dude, you think that's bad? My dad wasn't much better. And my last fuckin' boyfriend kicked me in the stomach until I miscarried. Yeah, I know it sucks but don't worry. I'm pregnant again, dude. Four months.

I'm bad-squirmy in my seat. Bridget decides to go back to the asshole who hit her. R. Sylvia comes down to ask if I would help out with Beth. In the delivery room Twack Jack and Echo are arguing out of control. He is yelling at her in between painful contractions.

Twack Jack: Echo, you don't understand. Why do you think I want to leave? Fuck, I'm doing this for you. I just want to go back to our room and make sure our stuff's safe. And I don't trust my bike in this hospital. Some doctor will probably steal it and I don't want to miss my SSI appointment tomorrow morning.

Echo: What a fuckin' asshole you are, Johnny. You ought to check a mirror and get a good look at yourself. You selfish bastard. No doctor is going to steal your motherfuckin' bike. Can't you just see some doctor racing around here on your bike, popping wheelies in the hall? And who gives a shit about our room right now? And why don't you call the guy at welfare and tell him you just had a baby? Fuuuuuck! Unh.

Twack Jack leaves the hospital and doesn't return 'til the next morning. By then Echo is having full blown, screaming contractions. Johnny is spinning harder than when he left.

The doctor is not a nice man. He keeps hinting that Echo is no good because she's a welfare case. The nurses give Beth oxygen in between the contractions. Thinking that no one is looking, Johnny tries to sneak the mask away and take a hit. At 10:35 a.m., Echo's daughter, Amber, arrives. At 10:40, Twack Jack asks the doctor for the hemostats that were used to tie the umbilical cord because he needs a new roach clip.

Saturday

R. Sylvia and Beth are ready to leave for New York, but Twack Jack is nowhere to be found. He's out getting high. Echo is disappointed with his drug habit but she thinks that he might as well have a little fun while he still can. R. Sylvia is vacillating between calling the cops and going out to find Twack Jack so she can kill him herself. He finally arrives on Monday morning, depressed because his bike got stolen.

> **Twack Jack:** You know, I hope this is a sign that there will be a happy ending to this story. I'm ready to mow the garage and paint the lawn.

At the airport I start calling "Echo" Beth, hoping that her days on the street are dead.

Winter

When they are not arguing, Beth and Twack Jack spend their time looking through mail order catalogues for things to buy. They are going to get an apartment as soon as Johnny finds a job. Beth's GA check and food stamps go to her mom for rent, cigarettes, and food. There's about $20 left over at the end of the month and that's spent on diapers.

Spring

Beth sends me a check, money taken from some GA savings. It is return bus fare for Johnny, who is in San Francisco on "family business." I promise to look for him. Two days later, Paul, the open-sore-snorting-speed-king, calls. He is despondent and can't understand why he's homeless again.

> **Paul:** It's Twack Jack's fault that I'm curbin' it. The greedy motherfucker's slammin' a gram a day. He slammed our dope deal away. By the way, you know anyone who wants to buy some speed?

Sunday

Twack Jack calls. He's ready for the ticket home.

> **Jim:** Did you take care of your "family business?"
>
> **Twack Jack:** Fuck family business. The only reason I came out here was to get way from that house and her bitchy and manipulative mom. I've been on a hell of a constant tweek with Bridget. She's eight months pregnant, still slammin' like a mothafucka. Damn, I've had some great thoughts. I think now I understand what most people could only dream of. No, I need drugs in my veins and I want to get my bike back.
>
> **Jim:** I thought it was stolen.
>
> **Twack Jack:** No, it's in a pawn shop. I lied.

This boy does not inspire trust. Echo asked me not to give him his ticket until he was on the bus, so we arrange to meet at the bus station. He never shows.

One week later

Twack Jack calls collect. He says he is in the hospital because he got hit by a car. LIE. I heard he was out looking for drugs, got in a fight over a bad deal, and got a one and a half inch blade stuck in him seven times. We finally meet up and I put him on the bus back to New York. Good-bye, Johnny. Good luck, Beth.

Summer

Beth: I'm pregnant again. This time it's Johnny's. I'm sorta happy about it all, 'cept he has no job and he's not going to his NA meetings and I don't trust him. My mom says he's drinking — sneaking Vodka from the bottle and refilling it with water. She's not too happy about all this. He thinks she's a royal bitch and wants to split. Maybe I would go with him if I had to. I don't know, he can be so immature and careless. He threw Amber up in the air when he shouldn't have. I'm due at the end of January and I'm afraid to tell him that I want to break up. There would be a scene and I don't know what would happen. Guess my plans have changed about school. Guess it's back to the same ol' same ol' for me.

Two weeks later

Beth says things are better. I'm not convinced. Everything she says is "just all right." Things are improving with her mom. She likes being pregnant. Twack Jack may get a job. Beth is hoping that the baby will be good for Johnny and help guide him toward a better life.

Early August

Beth is flustered, upset.

Beth: He's pushed me around one too many times, so I got pissed and threw his clothes out on the front lawn. My mom lost it and kicked his sorry ass out. I kinda miss him and I kinda don't. Guess I have no idea what I want, 'cept to get in a car and drive out to California. My plan is that I'll move back to San Francisco after the baby is born and work the telephone services awhile, at least until I get my own place.

Later, I walk by a car on 16th Street, door wide open. This guy with a rose tattoo on his back is fucking Bridget and slamming dope into her leg at the same time. I want to yell across the country to Beth that this will be her future if she becomes Echo again. Instead I write her a letter to lift her spirits.

February

Beth: Guess what, Jim. I had another girl. She's really cute! I named her Julie.

April

Beth is alone most of the day with the two girls. She has registered for computer repair school in the fall.

Beth: It's difficult and boring. I like my mom but I can't live with her. My little brother is a pain in the ass Ninja-wanna-be. My dad is trying to be nice, I guess.

It's hard to tell. He's always been better with machines than with his daughter. He fixed up his old car and gave it me. Now I drive to the malls and hope to meet somebody, except I'm too fat. I'm through with Twack Jack. He still doesn't get it that I don't want to be with him. He's going nowhere-cooking-cheesesteaks-fast.

October

Beth's been phoning a lot, mostly about her loneliness or a problem with school. She doesn't want to fix computers anymore. She whines that she doesn't know what she wants to do with her life and feels that she never has. She hates the suburbs, has no friends, argues with her mom too much, and feels stuck. Beth is dreaming only good dreams of the street, of Dave, of the lobby of the West Hotel, of being thin, and (of course) of shooting (tweek).

Her "asshole" stepfather is out of prison. He is remarried and works as a social worker. He drives up every Sunday to pick up her little brother for the day (visitation rights). She hates to think about what they might be doing together. Twack Jack lives in a boarding house and got a job stocking shelves in a discount store. Beth doesn't have much to do with him except on weekends, when she might bring the girls to the mall to see him. She watches TV a lot and saw Dave a couple of times — still getting famous on some talk show. I try to encourage her to get through this difficult period. I tell her that she should push herself more in English, that she could be a writer.

The phone conversation

Beth: Hello, it's Beth. I'm going to take a photo course and I need your advice. I got your postcard and want to hear about your trip to LA.

She asks me about the other kids. I tell her straight-up that I am seeing most of them die in front of me. The only healthy ones are in jail. I tell her I am not trying to scare her but am just being honest. I sense that she's happy. She is seeing somebody, a friend of a friend from school. Her two little daughters are doing fine. Amber is climbing stairs. (A baby cries in the background.)

She doesn't ask about Dave but I bring him up to tell her that he's in a jonesin' period. Simultaneously, I realize that he's now a full time junkie, that he's gone. Beth is also killing him off in her mind. Good-bye, Dave.

Winter

Beth thinks she has to quit school. She says she can't keep up with the homework, housework, the lack of money and sleep.

One year later

Beth: Hello, it's me, Echo, or Beth, or whatever. I got a job working as a data entry clerk. Mom's tired of my mess so I moved down to the basement. It's all right there. More room for me and the girls. Got my own phone. It takes me a week of work to pay for Dave's collect calls. He tells me that he loves me so much that he would move to New York, go into drug rehab, and become a father to my children. Ian has been calling, wanting me back as Echo, promising he will buy me an ice cream cone whenever I want. He swears he will help me make it in Hollywood this time.

July

Beth: My boss is an idiot! He thinks he knows everything but half the time I'm reading him the instructions. Got a few friends at work. They all think I'm funny. A couple of guys have asked me out. One's rather nice and he's a single dad. I met him in the McDonald's playground. I like his kid and I kinda like him. He's around 35, real normal. His hair is thinning. Turns out we have a lot in common, mostly about our dads. He and I can talk for hours about how unemotional they

are. His father fixes lawn mowers and my dad fixes cars, so we sit around on the porch and talk about the lawnmower parts on the ground and the cars jacked up in the driveway, while our own kids are running through the sprinklers. It makes me feel good and I know I'm almost home.

Christmas time

Jim: How are you?

Beth: (Hey, hey, hey, leave my purse alone!) I don't have many ornaments for the tree. I'm going to wait 'til they go on sale, maybe even buy an artificial one. I hate killing trees. Next year I'm going to shop in July. Yeah, everything is looking up. I have my own apartment and pictures to put up on the walls. The girls have a bunk-bed which they love and a big bedroom to tear apart. They love to make the worst messes. The kitchen is large enough for my three chairs and a card table. I even learned how to make meat loaf.... (Girls!) The living room has two end-tables and lamps, a Lazy-Boy and a ragged couch. It's all second hand Salvation Army kind of stuff, but it's fine for me. (Julie, stop pickin' on your older sister. I can't believe you. Get back in bed, c'mon.) The neighborhood is okay. No one is hanging out on the street corners and nice people live around here. It's safe for the girls.

Beth screams at Amber and Julie to get along with each other.

Beth: Hell, my place is a wreck. It's Amber's birthday and I'm making cupcakes for day care and a cake for the family party on Saturday. (Amber, get that out of your mouth!) Jim, she was eating wax. It's hard to find the time to clean. I decided I need a wife. There's a really cute guy at work who asked me to dance with him at the Christmas party. Guess what, I can't dance. I wish I could find somebody to marry me quick and get it over with.

There is crying in the background. Beth tries again to get her kids to stop hitting each other.

Beth: I swear I love them and will not kill them, but I'm going crazy. I even seriously considered letting Johnny move in with us. He says he wants to be near the girls. I think he thinks that we still have chance. I don't. He pushes me to the limit. There are too many things about him that bug me. Like why does he have to wear surfing shorts with work boots in the winter? It's like wearing a down jacket and underwear. (Stop that please. Stoppp.)

I just want a roommate, help with the children, and some money for rent. I want to go back to school and get my degree in business. (Amber, come here and I will help you. Don't!)

My family is helping. My father gives me money, and my grandmother and aunt are baby-sitting. Every day that I'm on my own and don't live at my mom's, like, I love them all more and more. Still, if I'm around my family too much I get wacko. Anybody would feel that way. There is no privacy with them and they like to get together all the time and celebrate something.

I was never really good at the family/social thing, which is why I think I liked the street and Dave so much. There was freedom there. It was special, the way we put up with each other. There was no separating Dave and Echo. We really were like twins. We fed into each other's stories, especially his bullshit ones. Like how he's going to die in six months. But now I figure I'm different than Dave. I found my freedom in another way. I like having a place to brush my teeth and my own bank account and a kitchen without cockroaches. I really do want to go back to school and get a degree.

Jim: Do you still dream about Dave?

Beth: No, not much. But I do keep having this bad nightmare, where I'm in California without the girls and all I want to do is get back home to them. But I can't, 'cause all my stuff's been ripped off and I'm stuck with Dave, living in some thrashed hotel room, depressed, hungry, jonesin', and ready to kill him over a quarter of a gram of speed. Then I wake up and I feel so depressed and bad that I think I can't get out of bed. But usually I can remind myself not to worry, that it's like Dave said, it's only a story, none of it is real, and there'll be a happy ending. (GIRLS, GIRLS, STOP THAT RIGHT NOW!) Good-bye, Jim....

Dave and the producer

Ian is always the same. He is like a happy, upbeat, semi-nice, drunk uncle from Australia.

Ian: Jim, things are good now. I'm a producer. I put a show together in three days. I do shows like, "My mom is trying to steal my kids — the battle over Brittany." The last one I did was about this radio talk show host who thinks all the homeless people should be put to sleep. I staged a riot for that one. It was all set up to look so bloody real. It's sweeps time and I make some good money doin' it. Right now I'm pitching one about this seventy pound lobster that a restaurant was going to cook, but because of this huge protest the restaurant took the lobster and put it back in the tank and made it their mascot. Now people are protesting that it's cruel to keep the lobster in a tank and that it should be put on a plane back to Maine and let go. But now there's also a protest from some group that wants to eat the bloody thing. It's sick.

The shows I set up with Dave are different. I've done thirty six with him and with each one the ratings have gone through the roof. Some people say I exploit him, but you know that's not true. Dave wants to be on TV. You know him and his mission to save the world. This way I get to do good work and the public gets some entertainment and hears the truth. Plus, Dave's become a sex symbol. I'm not kidding. Little girls from the suburbs are sending him letters with naked pictures. Just think, ten years ago everyone wanted to take me to court over all these stories about the bad things I supposedly had done. But now you can see how much good I'm doing.

The TV show

The camera pans across to Dave, trying to show him walking "naturally" down Hollywood Boulevard, his head hung low, his mouth way open. Because of sadness? Drugs? Is Dave dying?

Voice-over.

Host: This is Tweeky Dave. He's 19 and it's amazing that he is still alive. He's a drug addict, a former prostitute, plus he's dying of leukemia. He lives on the streets of Hollywood. He is the epitome of those we call "street kids." Dave is a legend who lives in the gutters of America. Many of you have written or called about Tweeky Dave, offering him money, food, and a place to live. You may be asking why Dave is still on the street. Well, when we return we will answer some of those questions, plus we will also hear from our three guests, all of whom want to thank Dave personally for saving their lives. So don't go away, we'll be right back.

Fade to commercial. Fade in clapping.

Dave is dressed in multi-colored overalls. His hair is bleached blond and long. A blue bandanna is tied around his head, and the word "tweek" is written on the brim of his baseball cap. A red bandanna is tied around the ankle of one of his high black boots. He has lots of make up on and a heavy lock is pulling on his ear lobe. His eyes are almost wrinkled shut. The way-too-earnest host interviews Dave, who likes the attention and responds with intelligent drama, as the TV camera focuses on the rotten stumps of his teeth.

Host: Dave, perhaps you can remind our audience how you ended up on the street.

Dave: My father raped me, then shot me in the stomach when I was nine. He left me at the hospital. I haven't seen my parents since. When I got better, I split from there and hitchhiked to Hollywood because I thought I was the one, you know, the one true rock and roll star. All I found there was a little love and a life of prostitution.

Host: The question is, Dave, since you have received all these offers of help, how has your life changed?

Dave: Well, I'm basically working to help other kids get off the streets and do more with their lives. And right now I am not strung out. I've been clean for a while and I have a place to live. But you gotta understand, the middle class dream of living in a home and being happy is culture shock to me. It blows me away. I mean, if the average kid in America watches as much TV as I have, no wonder they're all screwed up.

Host: Dave, you're obviously intelligent. Why can't you get it together now and work for a living?

Dave: Just look at me. I'm not able-bodied. I have a record. I don't have a resumé. You see, the streets are all I've ever known. It's not like I can go into McDonald's and ask them for a job. I mean, they won't even let me use their bathroom.

Host: When we return, Tweeky will be joined by three young women who saw him on TV and then wrote in to thank him and us for saving their lives....

Fade to commercial.

Host: Let me introduce Mallory Skidmore, Matilda Weathersby, and Kelly Walters.

These names are obviously made up. I recognize Mallory. She is Stony Beth, and Matilda is Li'l Bit. Kelly might be real. The camera pans across their handwriting as they read excerpts of letters they had supposedly sent to Dave. Mallory reads dramatically and Matilda is crying.

Mallory: I wanted to write because I gave up drugs after I saw Dave on TV.

Matilda: I, I, oh, I owe it all to Dave. He picked me up and literally carried me to a shelter to get me help. He....

Kelly: I grew up in a nice family. My parents did everything to send me to college. Now that I'm at the University of Virginia, and after seeing Tweeky Dave on one of your programs, I decided that I am going to get a degree in social work so I can help street kids.

Clapping. Fade to commercial.

The audience is asked to speak into a microphone the roving host carries with him. Most of their questions and comments are directed to Dave. The first speaker's eyes are wet from crying. She looks like Mia, another set up by Ian.

Audience Member #1: Dave, I really care. I really mean it from the heart. I will tell people about you and do everything possible to help you....

Clapping.

Audience Member #2: My question is to Dave. Don't you think you need new goals? On some level, aren't you wasting your life? How does it feel to have all these people love you so much, and yet you are still on the street?

People nod their heads with approval.

> **Dave:** It gets to me. I worry about all my friends who have AIDS, and all the rest
> who probably will die before they're 30. That's why I'm planning to go back to
> school, so I can become more of a voice for all the homeless people out there.
> See, you all don't know how hungry we are, and it's not just for food. Sometimes
> we're hungry for just a simple "hello." I mean, do you realize what real loneliness
> and rejection feels like, especially when you're dying?
>
> **Host:** Let me introduce a man who has dedicated his life to children on the street,
> giving them food, jobs, and a place to stay. Please welcome Ian Bostwick, who
> runs an organization called "This Way Out."

*Ian talks about how to be a positive, loving, and healthy role model. A 1-800 number is
flashed on the screen so that anyone who is interested can send money for his "youth
program."*

Fade to commercial. It's the end of TV for me.

Easter

The phone rings. A computer voice asks if I will accept "a collect call from" —
pause — and Dave says, "Dave." The voice requests, "if so press 1 or say yes now...."
The computer thanks me.

> **Dave:** Hey Jim, what's up? I just got out of jail. I got me a black eye and
> a broken jaw. You know, gang bangers. I'm packing a .22. I'll see you in a few days.
> I'm coming up to Frisco. Gotta go now and fight this guy. Bye.

Hollyweird

Dave is staying in a large apartment building-turned-squat called "The House of Pain."
People with guns are on the fire escape. It's very loud and frighteningly intense
there. Behind a window I see some scary looking pumped-up tweeker jumping up and
down, threatening to hurt me because he thinks I'm a cop. There is a barricade across
what was once the front door. I do not try to cross it. Instead I yell my message into
a slot, telling someone to tell Dave that I was here looking for him, and to meet me in
the Fame. I sit in the café for two days, waiting. Finally Dave arrives. There is no
dangling lock from his ear. His earlobe now forms an upside-down V, just like Echo's.
His face and hands are caked with dirt.

> **Dave:** What's up, daddy-o? Is the bitch dying without me? I'm in a "jonesin-for-her"
> kind of mood and I need a change from Hollyweird. It's getting to me, Jim. Listen,
> I'm hungry and if you want to save money, buy me two cups of coffee and an order
> of fries, with a side of blue cheese.

Dave has no teeth so he sticks his fingers into the bowl of blue cheese dressing,
leaving the fries for me. I show Dave the dummy for my book. He reads every bit of
writing, looks at every picture, and asks no questions. When he's done, he wipes
his hands on the book.

> **Dave:** Dude, sometimes remembering is much more fun than livin' any reality of
> today. Gotta go, Jim. There's this new little Deadhead chick who just rolled into
> town, and she's promising to get me high.

For a year and a half I imagine Dave is dead

Most of the time I have no idea how or where Dave really is. I keep hearing stories that he's dead or almost there. Last week, the director of an "AIDS and Youth at Risk" study called to say that he heard that Dave had OD'd. Today, Dave calls.

Dave: Hey dad, I've been clean for months. I'm, like, so healthy I'm beginning to think I may live. Dude, I weigh a hundred and sixty now. I've been living out in the valley with a Christian family, but thinkin' 'bout goin' back to Hollywood and tryin' to get me some AIDS. I figure we're all dying. Nikki Pain is. So is Ziggy. Heard straight-up they both got it one hundred percent. I figure the only reason I ain't got it is 'cause they all used to let me shoot up first. They must have thought I was sick already, since I'm so ugly and dead looking. Wait, hold on, Jim.

I hear some guy talking to Dave in a wild way. It gets louder.

Dave: Look, I have to go kick somebody's ass. I'll call you later.

Early February

Dave calls from a pay phone in a nursing home.

Dave: I broke my leg and fractured my hip skateboarding. I tell everybody that it was a motorcycle accident. Figure I got to be like James Dean in people's minds, somehow. So, guess what? I got all my stumps pulled and I'm getting fitted for a new set of teeth next week. Dude, when I get out of here I'm gonna go to USC, no shit. For now, I got to get me a better business manager for the talk show thing. Ian only gets me two hundred dollars. I figure I'm worth five. Damn, Jim, just when you think we could talk, some guy gets in line. Got to go. Call me tomorrow.

Two days later he's gone.

July, call from a phone booth, Sunset Boulevard

Jim: Dave, where have you been? I've been worryin' about you.

Dave: Dad, you worry too much. I got it going on, a hustle here and a hustle there. Lately, I've been an extra on some film about life under the freeway. They needed real people who were dying. I'm gonna be their poster boy. I got twenty five bucks a day, free food, plus I get to hang out with movie stars. Dude, I look so bad I'm giving up on getting false teeth. That way I can have a new lie and say I'm 60 and I used to hang out with Kerouac and Kesey. Some producer even promised to help publish one of the songs I wrote about Echo and me. Maybe this time . . . .

Jim: You still want her, huh?

Dave: Stick the needle in and feel the rush begin. Do a bag a day to keep the pain away. Dude, you gotta understand, it's not the same without her. She's in my blood. I figure that without Echo I have nothing to live for, so I might as well love her, even if it kills me. Have you talked to her, Jim? Does she still dream about being a junkie with me or does she like making cookies in suburbia? What's her number, Jim?

Jim: Dave, what about that family you were living with?

Dave: Fuck that suburban shit. I tried taking showers. I decided I like being dirty and strung out. Fuck, I'm in so much pain, the scar over my stomach hurts. I had a doctor check me out, and he told me I have only a few months to live. What's Echo's number, Jim?

I give it to him for the millionth time.

Dave: Listen, I gotta split and find me God. I hear he's 'round the corner at Rock and Roll Denny's. It's that China White I want to slam up my arms.

Before hanging up, he sings a few lines to the tune of "If I only had a brain" from the Wizard of Oz.

Dave: If I only had a vein.... Later dude.

One month later, a "Board and Care" home

Dave: Jim, they scraped me up off the sidewalk to get me here. My white count is down to 45,000. I have hepatitis and cirrhosis of the liver. Dude, I straight-up have two years to live.

Jim: What about your leukemia?

Dave: Dude, I'm dying. What difference does it make? But I ain't stressin', and you know why?

He sings a few lines in a bad Woody Guthrie voice:

Dave: I figure everything dies, that's a fact, and maybe everything that dies, someday comes back....

Guess what? I just got off the phone with Echo. She seems to be finally softening to my advances. I'm thinking I may actually get laid. The way I see it, Echo has slammed the door in my face so hard and so many times that it keeps bouncing right back open. Dude, she even reminded me of that one Valentine's Day when I dedicated all of Bon Jovi to her. I mean, I've been so crazy in love with that bitch for so long, Jim. What do you think about me going to New York? Echo's mom said she would take care of me if I ever did, and then I could help Echo and go straight and be the father of her children.

Hey, I just remembered, I gotta call Echo back. What's her number, Jim? I forgot to tell her about the two new tats I'm gonna put on my arm: "Echo" and "Sworn to fun, Loyal to one." I'll call you later, Jim. Promise. I love you, man.

Hospital, October 22

The next time I hear from Dave it's two months later. He is in Rancho Los Amigos Hospital.

> **Dave:** It's bad, Jim. I'm swollen-yellow. My liver is shot. I have hepatitis A, B, C, and D, and maybe E. The doc says that I only got six months to live.
>
> **Jim:** Dave, you've been dying for years. I don't know what to believe anymore.
>
> **Dave:** Truth is, I don't either. I feel caught myself, like I'm stuck in between right and wrong. It's so hard to explain on the phone, Jim. All I want to do is to sit and write it all down on some paper for you.
>
> **Jim:** Dave, I don't know if I want to know the truth anymore. It's probably all the truth, isn't it?
>
> **Dave:** The motherfuckin' truth is that if I have to die here, I hope I kick it with a hell a lot of morphine goin' up my veins. I'm fuckin' bored, Jim. They say they're going to put me in a nursing home in a week or so. Fuck, if I do get released and I don't like the god damn place, I promise you I'm AWOLing it to Hollywood. Shit yeah, dude, I'll find me a gram of some down dope and get me to Oasis alley so I can straight-up slam it all.

He laughs.

> **Dave:** Fuck yeah, then I'll crawl what's left of my sorry, orphaned life out on to Hollywood Boulevard and OD right there, fast and loud, on top of James Dean. Hope the motherfuckin' street gets stained yellow from the piss an' tears of all my friends. Maybe somebody will even spray paint a star for me on that motherfuckin', lyin' "boulevard of dreams." Jim, do me a favor and send me some Kerouac and Bukowski books, paper, and some envelopes and stamps. Then I promise I will write you back and blow your mind with the truth. Okay? I gotta go talk to the social worker. Send me the paper, okay?

I send the stuff and later I receive from Dave a note:

Guest list for my funeral

Anybody who wants to come (except for Tiny Waller and Doug)

Echo and her kids

Echo's mom

Jim and Susan and the kid

Lupé

Cookie

Ziggy (I guess)

Cruise and Crash

Pops (just in case I want to get high on my way to hell)

Anne-Marie (but not Nigel, her boyfriend)

Freckie, Sue, Tori, Casper, Hippie Chick, Psycho, not Tank

(no assholes except me allowed)

Tweeky Michelle, Boss Bitch, Coma, Playboy, Destiny, Weedhopper

Pup Dog, Drunk Ray, Shorty, Hippie Dave, and Li'l Bit,

of course Doper Molly, Perry, Wea, Crow, Universe, Blade,

Officers Ruby and Moore

Mindy the Counselor

and Gabe if he hadn't died of AIDS,

Cher (what the fuck)

Dylan, Keith, and Sid and Nancy (if she promises not to whine)

Axel and Slash, Yoko Ono, Jim Morrison, Neil Young, Jerry Garcia,

Johnny Thunder, Johnny Ramone, and Johnny Cash

Madonna and Michelle Shocked (I would fuck either)

Mozart, Beethoven, and definitely Mahler

Bob Marley, Mick Jagger, Iggy, Warhol, Lou Reed,

Willy Nelson, Loretta Lynn, Gore Vidal, Stephen King, Henry Miller,

Ursula Leguin, John Lennon, Dostoevsky, Marx, Lenin, and Freud,

Kerouac (he's pretty much God — he can say the prayer),

Allen Ginsberg, Robert Frank, Picasso, Henry Rollins

Trent from Nine Inch Nails

Ken Kesey, Neal Cassady, John Steinbeck,

James Dean, James Brown, Elvis (the fat fuck)

All corrupt politicians

Jesus Christ and Buddha

and all my enemies, including (maybe)

my mom and dad.

November 4, fucking pissed, hospital

Jim: What's up Dave? How are you doin?

Dave: Fuck, Jim, I'm tired of people asking me that question. I'm fuckin' sick a lot. And I don't want to fuckin' talk so much, so leave me alone, okay?

Jim: I'm sorry Dave. I was just tryin' to....

Dave: Stop tryin'. It ain't fuckin' worth it dude. Bye.

I call him right back and someone else answers, who yells out in a thick eastern European accent, "Day-vud, Day-vud." Dave gets back on the phone.

Dave: I'm sorry, man, for being such an asshole, but I just can't talk too much. Call my doctor, he'll tell you everything. I signed a release so you can get any fuckin' information you want. Listen, I'm sick, I gotta go throw up, okay? Later.

Dave has never apologized for anything before.

Cheap trick

It's difficult for me to explain, even at this point, with all that I know of Dave, that somehow this feels like one of his lies. He would never die. All I've been able to confirm is that Dave is in the hospital liver unit. Finally, I speak to a doctor who doesn't know anything about Dave. I try to impart some humanity into the situation to protect him.

Jim: Hello doctor, my name is Jim Goldberg. I am a photographer who is doing a book about street kids, and, well, one of your patients, David Miller, is a friend of mine. He also happens to be one of the main people in the book. David told me to call you, to see how he is doing? You see, he has no family and it's difficult for me, being up here. I think he's signed a release so you can tell me....

Doctor Burstein: Yes, yes, Mr. Goldberg, David Miller's liver is in the advanced form of the disease and is mostly destroyed. He has hepatitis B, C, and D.

Jim: What can I do? I plan on coming down in a few weeks. I mean, how long does he have?

Doctor Burstein: His overall prognosis is extremely poor. It is difficult to say in these cases. Probably a year, maybe two.

Jim: What will happen to him in the meantime? He can't stay in the hospital forever, can he?

Doctor Burstein: Although I'm not sure, I think we're in the process of placing him in a nursing home. We're probably just waiting for an opening. You should speak to the social worker who is in charge of his case.

He gives me the number.

Jim: Doctor, Dave has had a drug problem. If he should go out and do heroin again, would it kill him?

Doctor Burstein: No, it's too late for that.

Second week of November

Dave: I'm feeling better, but I'm tired of kickin' it here. They've been saying for weeks they're thinkin' of putting me in a nursing home. Hell, I don't know if I can wait that long. It's driving me fucking crazy. I'm telling you dude, I need my freedom. I read every fuckin' book you sent me, man, plus every motherfuckin' "Readers Digest" that these ol' fucks have lying around here. Fuck, I can't watch TV anymore. It's making me god damn stupid. I'm even sick of seeing myself on the re-runs. And all the motherfuckin' doctors want to do is run tests on me. I don't know what they're goin' to find out. We all know I'm gonna die. I bet those fuckers can't wait to cut me up and see how I work. Dad, do me a favor and don't let the doctors get to me, okay? Just throw my body in a dumpster on the boulevard, pour gasoline on it, and straight-up burn me to hell right there. Okay?

Long pause.

Dave: Jim, do you think I should tell Echo what's up, that it's getting too dark for me to see?

He sings his version of Axel doing Dylan:

Dave: Knock, knock, knocking on heaven's door....

He lets out a twisted laugh.

Dave: Hell, the chick might even fuck me if she found out. What's her number, Jim? Wait, hold on. Does anybody got a pen or a pencil or anything, puuleese? Thanks. This time I won't lose it, Jim. I'm writing it in a Bible. Gotta go dude, they're going to run some more tests on me. See ya. Peace.

November 17, happy ending

Dave: Dude, everything's cool at the beginning. Me and Echo are alone in a room in Hollywood, buzzed off some killer shit. We're both trippin' 'cause it's so fine, like we're family again. Hell, maybe we're even in love. Who knows? Who cares? 'Cause I think we're getting ready to finally fuck. No shit, dude. I'm even, like, taking off my clothes and shit, and then all of a sudden everything goes dark. Then I realize the bitch has straight-up killed me dead.

And then I'm, like, falling, and falling, and falling until I end up in this hot waiting room outside of hell with a TV on. She's on it, getting some motherfuckin' award for fuckin' killing me. And I'm like sketching so fuckin' hard, all pissed and shit. And that's when I usually wake up, lying in this god damn hospital bed, listening to all these sick poor souls dying all around me. And I realize, hey, if I have to fry in hell so that my baby can go on, that's cool. I can live with that.

Late afternoon, November 20

Jim: Hi Dave. What's up?

Dave: Can't talk, Jim. They're taking me to the ICU. Good-bye, I love you.

When I call the next morning I get the man with the eastern European accent who doesn't understand what I am saying. Finally a nurse gets on the line.

Nurse: Mr. Goldberg, we have been trying to reach you all morning. I'm sorry to have to be telling you this, but David Miller died last night in the ICU. If you want, you can speak to the doctor. I'll go get him. He's right here. Hold on please.

Her words crash through my brain. I go numb.

Doctor Burstein: Yes. I'm sorry. It took me by surprise also. When I saw him yesterday, the diarrhea had slowed down and his spirits seemed fine, but later in the day another doctor found fluid in his belly. So it must have been a perforated bowel. His blood pressure was low, there was kidney failure, he went into shock, code blue, ventrichia tachycardia. It's so hard to predict with these liver disease cases. The bleeding and infection is what usually kills them. I can't be sure though, in David's case, unless I do an autopsy. I'm curious about how he managed to survive so long, looking the way he did.

Jim: Well, I know that Dave would not want that. He asked me to have his body cremated. Perhaps you could direct me to the person I could speak with to deal with arranging, uh, the ....

Doctor Burstein: Yes, well, we all thought that you, ah, that he was an orphan. It's funny. The social worker just got a call from Texas. We found out that Dave has a father and sister.

This news hits like another concussion to my system. I am immediately afraid for Dave. How do I know that his father and family aren't what he has described? I can't assume that Dave will not be left to rot. I want to find out what's going on. My only hope is to leave my number for the family to call, just in case.

Daddy

I leave the recorded message on my machine for the longest time. The voice of a frail older man says, "Hello, Mr. Goldberg, my name is Jeffrey Marrs and I am David Miller's father. Could you please call me back here in Texas at.... I phone Dave's dad.

Father: Hello? Yes, I wanted to thank you for being such a good friend to our son, David. I don't know if you realize how very dear he was to us all. He's had a bed here whenever he wanted. When his momma and I found him so many years ago, so sick, we knew then that we would adopt him and give him our best. We took such good care of that boy, you see. We both have become sick over him. We are good Christian people who would never do what he said on TV. It's just that he couldn't march to the drum beat at home. Yes, David was indeed loved.

He leaves no room for further conversation.

Father: Well, you must excuse me, I'm not feeling very well right now. So if you wouldn't mind, please call my daughter, Peggy Romer, at 806....

When I phone, Dave's brother-in law answers.

Brother-in-law: I didn't know Dave directly, but from what I do know, he has done some pretty horrible things to his family. Evidently, the person his family knew and the person Dave was, were two different people.

He passes the phone to his wife, Dave's sister.

Sister: What can you tell me about David?

This is weird. Shouldn't she know more than I do?

Jim: That's what I was going to ask you.

She takes a long drag on a cigarette.

Sister: A lot of what David said on TV was just not true. He was not abused. He was not shot. My daddy never even owned a gun. My family are good, God-fearing people who worried and prayed for David everyday.

Jim: Then why did Dave say all those things?

Pause. Cigarette.

Sister: David was a very confused boy, a very sad young man. Evidently, he was more at home out there on the street than he ever was here with us.

Jim: Why? What happened?

Sister: It's an old story that I'm, frankly, quite tired of thinking about.

Jim: Dave told many different stories so it's so hard to know whether....

Sister: We were fraternal twins. We were both deserted in a hospital and adopted at the same time by our new parents. I was okay, so they took me home with them. But David was born with severe birth defects and spent the first two years of his life in the hospital. The county did experimental surgery on him. He had to have multiple cystostomies. You see, he was born without stomach muscles so he couldn't sit up on his own. Plus he had liver problems and who knows what else. He was a mess and no one expected him to live to be 18.

Poor momma had to teach him on how to go to the bathroom. My daddy has arthritis in his hands so bad because he took such good care of David. I'll tell you, they loved us like we were their own. But even with all of this love, and us being brought up in the church, David still had a troubled childhood.

Jim: But why him and why not you?

Sister: My guess is that David never could distinguish between reality and his dreams. I think this was because of his psychological and physical problems. They got in the way of everything. He stuck out so much that he never grew up. He ended up being a very confused boy who always needed more than anyone could give him.

Jim: When did you last see him?

She lights another cigarette.

Sister: In person? He was home about ten years ago, right before momma died. He was with a girl. They left a week after they got here. We had no idea where they went. Then, a few years ago we got a call from someone in our church who had seen David on a TV talk show. They asked if that was our David. Sure enough it was, and that's how we knew he was still alive. For the last two years, David has been calling daddy and promising that he was coming back home, and daddy could only ask, "How could you say all those things about your momma and I?" David would only answer, "Well, well, well…." You know, if you watched that program you might think that my parents were really bad people but they're not.

Listen, Mr. Goldberg, don't take what I'm about to say wrong. I am very sorry about my brother and what has happened to him. But he was like all those kids who can't face the music, you know. It's all about escapism. He ran away and chose his own life. He was a very confused boy.

She inhales and blows the smoke into the phone.

Sister: Perhaps he believed those things, as if somewhere in his own mind he thought he wouldn't actually be welcome at home. On some level though, I think David knew we loved him. It's all so sad and tragic.

Pause.

Sister: Whew, it's over 80 degrees here in Texas. It's too hot to be thinking about all this sad stuff.

Jim: Do you have plans for a funeral? We are going to have service in Hollywood for him. Perhaps you would like to come out for it?

Long sigh.

> **Sister:** We think that daddy may have had a heart attack. We have to wait until the tests come in. So my thoughts are that it wouldn't be a good idea to bring daddy to California for a funeral. I think it would make daddy feel guilty to see David lying there. It would be like a big slap in his face. No, I'd rather he wasn't involved in all the dark stuff of life. Anyway, don't you think David might be happier if he was taken care of by his friends, by those who are more like he was?
>
> **Jim:** Are you saying you want me to take care of his remains?
>
> **Sister:** Yes, that would be fine. I will send a letter to the hospital giving power of attorney to you. And please let me know if there is anything else we can do. We really do appreciate all your assistance. Good-bye.

I call them again and leave a message about the date of Dave's funeral. They never call back.

The real world

I remember that Dave had wanted to die fast — like a car-crashing beatnick going over a cliff — and loud — like some infamously unlucky rock-star-cum-addict who had slammed his last half gram of speed and drank his last bit of Wild Turkey while having a conversation about music and hope and playing feedback crashing guitar with a camel (straight) hanging from his mouth.

The service is in a sanitized Salvation Army youth center. The room is filled with adults and kids, who each tell stories about Dave. He illustrated his life to all of us with different parts of different stories, and so when we repeat them back to each other, the pieces don't really fit together. It's almost funny. All those lies and stories in one room add up to something close to the truth.

Everyone is crying. We all write notes to Dave and tie them on strings with balloons. We hold hands and let them go high above the boulevard. The whole thing is sappy, in a wonderful, happy-ending-kind-of-way. Dave deserved a happy ending. As the balloons disappear to the east, his funeral ends. A few kids tell me they're going to get high and dedicate the rush to Dave, hoping to meet him again on the other side. The rest of us drink Hi-C and eat Mister Chips cookies.

When I get home, I call Beth to fill her in on the ceremony. She can't really say much. She cries and has to hang up. Later she calls back.

> **Beth:** It figures that he came from middle class America and that his parents are God-fearing people who will pray for him but not even touch him or go to his funeral. I would've been there in a minute if I could, but you know I couldn't 'cause I had to work.
>
> I realize how much I miss him now that Dave's gone. He's taken a piece of my heart with him, stealing some of my memories of what's good about Hollywood.
>
> So, Jim, I've been sad all day thinking about Dave. You know, when I got home from work, I decided to watch some MTV to get my mind off of him. Well, there I am, looking at "Real World," and there's Dave, jumping up and down right in front of the camera where they're filming on Hollywood Boulevard.

Fade out.

Acknowledgements

Raised by Wolves was produced over a period of ten years, from 1985 to 1995, an arduous journey that required help and encouragement from many people. This project is, of course, dedicated to Tweeky Dave, Echo, and many friends who shared their stories and lives with me. I have given most of you pseudonyms to conceal your identities. I trust you know who you are: R. Sylvia and family, Marcos, Deion, Brad, Blade, Tank, Cookie, Ziggy, Rusty, Vyper, Stevie Kaos, Anne Marie, and all the rest of you curb-hugging rolling souls. You are the inspiration for this work, which is as much your doing as it is mine. Thanks.

I am indebted to the following people who have made this project possible: Philip Brookman of the Corcoran Gallery of Art, who became my brother-double, my collaborator on this book and exhibition, and who helped me to trust my vision; Lorelei Stewart, my assistant and friend, who kept everyone and everything in order in the midst of impossible chaos; Tony Tredway, who was at times my arms, legs, and courage; James Dawson, who took my scratchy negatives and made beautiful prints for the book and exhibition; David Ireland, whose vision, consideration, and understanding of this story were translated into the exhibition design; Jock Reynolds of the Addison Gallery of American Art, whose enthusiasm and respect helped launch the project; Walter Keller of Scalo, whose intellect, prescience, and courage are written all over this book; Hans Werner Holzwarth of Design pur, whose sharpened sense of design and smiling opinions brought the pieces together as one; Gerd Steidl and Gerd Schwab of Steidl, whose expertise enabled the printing of this book; and Martin Heller of the Zurich Museum of Design, whose intelligent curiosity brought the exhibition to Europe.

I especially want to thank Bill Delzell, Betsy K. Frampton, Ann Hatch, and Henrik Kam, whose support always came at the most critical moments, when it seemed I couldn't continue. You are angels. This book and exhibition were together made possible through the selfless support of many individuals, foundations, and corporate sponsors: the Glen Eagles Foundation; Molly White and the Gap Foundation; Terri L. Freeman, Renette Oklewicz, and the Freddie Mac Foundation; Lisa Lyons, Tim Peterson, and the Lannan Foundation; Avery Russell and the Carnegie Corporation of New York; J. Regan Mahoney, Peter Hogg, Troy Peters, and The Digital Pond; Theodore Adamstein and Chrome.

In addition, I want to thank the following individuals and institutions, whose foresight and generosity sustained my work through many years, preventing these pages from remaining blank: Art Matters; Sandra Berler; Gay Block; Pamela Bonino; Andrew Bundy and Karen Hansen; the California Arts Council; the California Tamarack Foundation; Capp Street Project; Rosemary Carroll and Janine Nadler; Creative Time; the Guggenheim Foundation; Brenda Hershey and Barry Fell; the Highlands Award; the Jaffe Award; the Kormans; Mike Light; Peter MacGill and Pace/MacGill Gallery; Lloyd and Ann Miller; the National Endowment for the Arts; Trip Van Noppen and Rivka Gordon; Robert Preston; Jed Emerson and the Roberts Foundation on Homelessness; Rose Steinman; Sam Yanes, Barbara Hitchcock, and the Polaroid Corporation; the T. B. Walker Foundation; and Washington Project for the Arts.

The production of this book and exhibition have been complex and multi-layered projects. I am indebted to all those people whose professional skills and trust in my work have been instrumental in making these projects possible. I want to thank David C. Levy, Jack Cowart, Susan Badder, Susan Rosenbaum, John Chappell, Joy Hallinan, Nancy LeRoy, Janet Solinger, Victoria Larson, Ken Ashton, Chan Chao, Julie Solz, Cindy Rom, Steve Brown, Joyce Peterson, Libby Rogers, Michelle Saffir, Sher King, and Paul Roth at the Corcoran Gallery of Art; the entire staff of the Addison Gallery of American Art; Sally Abugov; Alexandra Gübeli, Gaby Weiss, Helga Krempke, and Jürg Abegg at the Zurich Museum of Design; and Miriam Wiesel at Scalo. Numerous individuals and organizations have been crucial in the development of education and outreach programs that accompany the exhibition, including: Jennifer Nelson; Marian Wright Edelman and Donna Jablonski, Children's Defense Fund; Gary de Carolis, U.S. Department of Health and Human Services, Center for Mental Health Services; Maria Foscarinis, National Law Center on Homelessness and Poverty; Deborah Shore and Mark Lloyd, Sasha Bruce Youthwork; Debbie Riley, Operation Runaway; and Tracy Chamblin, National Clearinghouse on Runaway and Homeless Youth.

My appreciation and thanks is also extended to the many dedicated people and organizations I have worked with through the years, who help kids daily and who helped me in the most imaginative ways: Kathy Baxter Stern, San Francisco Child Abuse Council; Drs. Richard Brown and Bonnie Datell, San Francisco General Hospital; Dr. Norm

Carrey and L. Warde Laidman, the McAuley Institute; Diane
Doherty, CASSP Technical Assistance Center; Jonathan
French, Ed Vasgersian, Gary Harding, Dr. Ronnell Lewis, and
the staff of the San Francisco Youth Guidance Center;
Glenn Goldberg, California Consortium of Child Abuse
Councils; Clayton Golliher, Hope Chapel; Gary Griffen and
the Los Angeles Police Department; Judge Ronald
Greenberg; Larkin Street Youth Center; Mindi Levins, LAYN;
Cajetan Luna, West Hollywood Sheriff's Department;
Drs. Richard McKenzie and Gary Yates, Children's Hospital,
Los Angeles; Holly Pera and the San Francisco Police
Department Juvenile Division; Eric Rofes, Gabe Kruks,
and the Gay and Lesbian Community Service Center;
Boyd Stephens, San Francisco Medical Examiner;
Maureen See, Children's Garden; Francis Tauber, CASARC;
Dale Weaver, Teen Canteen; Judge Daniel Weinstein;
and Judge Roy Wonder.

I also must give special thanks to my family and
friends, who all supported me in a multitude of ways:
Stuart Alexander, F. J. Bolger, Amy and Daniel Brookman,
Cee Brown, Steven Buckingham, Bill B. Burke,
Bryan H. Burkhardt and Carolyn Eicher, Melissa Checker,
Robert Delpire, Jennifer Dowley, Doug Dubois, Robert Frank,
Griselia Flores, Hannah Frost, Scott Generick, Herbert and
Lillian Goldberg, Nan Goldin, Marion Goodell, Doug Hall,
Dennis Hearne, Meghan and Mary Ann Jenks, Mary Kaplan,
Carol Kismaric, Susan Kismaric, Andy Kivel, Bill Laven,
June Leaf, Jane Livingston, George LeGrady, Chip Lord,
Danny Lyon, Elaine Mayes, the Mayohs, Aengus McGiffin,
Eric McNatt, Susan Meiselas, the entire Miller clan,
Ken Miller, Weston Naef, Lorie Novak, Ronnie Ong,
Ilona Wiewiorra-Buller, David Pearson and Gravity Works,
Gilles Peress, Henri Peretz, Dede Peters, Sandra Phillips,
Paul Quintelian and Sean Mattingly, Elizabeth Radigoy,
John Randolph, Susan Schwartzenberg, Anastasia Shartin,
Alice Shaw, Jay Shanker and Sara Jane Rose, Gary Smith,
Oren Sreebny and Michelle Rudnick, Robert Sobieszek,
Louise Steinman and Lloyd Hamrol, David Levi Strauss,
Larry and Kelly Sultan, Bruce Tomb, Kerry Tremain,
Anne Tucker, Anne Walsh, the Wattenberg-Chase family,
and Tim Zgraggen.

Finally, to Susan Miller, my wise ol' backbone an' eyes,
and my daughter Ruby Sophia, it is our love and your
inspiration that nourished me and got me through it all.
Thank you.

Jim Goldberg

Raised by Wolves: Photographs and Documents of Runaways
by Jim Goldberg is organized by the Corcoran Gallery of Art and
the Addison Gallery of American Art, in collaboration with
the Zurich Museum of Design, and is curated by Philip Brookman,
curator of photography and media arts, the Corcoran Gallery of Art,
and Jock Reynolds, director, Addison Gallery of American Art.

Zurich Museum of Design
May 30 – July 30, 1995

The Corcoran Gallery of Art, Washington
September 16 – November 19, 1995

Addison Gallery of American Art, Andover
January 12 – March 24, 1996

Los Angeles County Museum of Art
March 13 – May 11, 1997

San Francisco Museum of Modern Art
June 19 – September 11, 1997

Southeast Museum of Photography, Daytona Beach
October 14, 1997 – January 9, 1998

Museum of Contemporary Photography, Chicago
January 24 – March 21, 1998

This book is made possible by a major grant from:
Glen Eagles Foundation

The exhibition and related programs are made possible
by major grants from:
Gap Foundation
Freddie Mac Foundation
Lannan Foundation
with additional support from:
Carnegie Corporation of New York
Glen Eagles Foundation
California Tamarack Foundation
The Digital Pond, San Francisco
Chrome, Washington

With the exception of the primary characters, the names of
those appearing in this book have been changed to protect their
identities. The handwritten texts are by homeless youth living
on the streets of San Francisco and Hollywood.

Photographs and text are copyright by Jim Goldberg.
All photographs are by Jim Goldberg, except pp. 44–45, 83,
114–115, 152–153, 175, 222–223, 240–241, and 279 by
Bill Delzell and Jim Goldberg; pp. 6–7 by Henrik Kam and
Jim Goldberg; pp. 4–5, 236–237, and 316 by Philip Brookman
and Jim Goldberg; and pp. 12, 13, 14, 19, 20, 21, 205, 208,
214, and 271, anonymous.

Edited by Philip Brookman and Jim Goldberg.
Designed by Jim Goldberg, Philip Brookman, and Hans Werner
Holzwarth, Design pur, Berlin, with assistance from Sally Abugov.
Production by Steidl, Göttingen.

Raised by Wolves is published by Scalo Zurich – Berlin – New York.
Head Office: Weinbergstrasse 22a, CH-8001 Zurich / Switzerland,
phone 41 1 261 0910, fax 41 1 261 9262. Distributed in North America
by D.A.P., New York City; in Europe and Asia by Thames and Hudson,
London; in Germany, Austria and Switzerland by Scalo.

Second Scalo Edition 1997
ISBN 1-881616-50-9

Printed in Germany